need to know?

Antique Marks

The Diagram Group

Collins

First published in 2006 by Collins
an imprint of
HarperCollins Publishers
77-85 Fulham Palace Road
London W6 8JB

www.collins.co.uk

A catalogue record for this book is available from the British Library

Series design: Mark Thomson

Created by: The Diagram Group
Contributing editors: Simon Adams, David Harding, Chris Osborn, Anna Selby
Designers: Anthony Atherton, Lee Lawrence, Ruth Shane
Picture research: Neil McKenna, Diana Philips, Patricia Robertson

ISBN 0 00 7205856

Colour reproduction by Colourscan, Singapore
Printed and bound by Printing Express Ltd, Hong Kong

ACKNOWLEDGEMENTS

Neil McKenna 8, 100, 122
Sandra Lipton 27, 28, 29, 30, 37, 38, 44, 54, 55, 57, 61, 62, 69, 70, 75, 79, 81
Daniel Bexfield 31, 71, 82
Bryan Douglas 32, 67, 76
Esford Pty 116
Mike Lemke 177

For their co-operation and assistance we would like to thank the following organisations:
The British Museum, Christie's, Grosvenor Museum, The London Library, Phoenixmasonry, Sotheby's

Contents

Introduction 6

1 **Precious metals** 8

Hallmarks on silver, gold and platinum 10–24

British Assay Offices: London, Edinburgh, York, Norwich, Exeter, Dublin, Newcastle, Chester, Glasgow, Birmingham and Sheffield 25–83

American gold and silver 84–85

African gold 86–87

Indian colonial gold and silver 88–89

Leading goldsmiths and silversmiths 90–94

Goldsmiths' and silversmiths' terminology 95–99

2 **Pewter and Sheffield Plate** 100

Old Sheffield Plate 102–109

Pewter 110–113

Precious metal working 114–121

3 **Ceramics** 122

Pottery and porcelain 124–126

Ceramic makers' marks: A to Z 127–148

Ceramic makers' marks: symbols 149–167

Leading pottery and porcelain manufacturers 168–173

Methods of construction 174–177

Surface work 178–179

Oriental porcelain 180–183

Ceramic terminology 184–188

Need to know more? 189

Index 190

Introduction

Do you ever attend car boot sales or browse in antique shops in search of bargains? Have you ever wished you knew more about your grandmother's silver spoon, or that old piece of china which has been around your home for so many years? Do you envy the experts' ability to identify and date such fascinating hand-me-downs? If the answer to any of these questions is yes, then *Collins need to know? Antique Marks* is for you.

Spanish chalice with repoussé and chased decoration, 1670

The book begins with a clear and thorough guide to the hallmarks stamped on British gold and silver since the Middle Ages, and those now found on platinum. The precious metals section continues with pages exclusively devoted to American, African and Asian gold and silver; a historical review of leading goldsmiths and silversmiths; and a glossary of the terminology currently used by the professionals.

The second section of the book looks at the quite different marks to be found on Old Sheffield Plate. A representative selection of pewter makers' marks is provided next, as an introduction to these once very common household wares. This section closes with an examination of some traditional techniques used in working with precious metals.

The final section of the book surveys the vast range of marks to be found on pottery or porcelain, both from Britain and the rest of Europe, and from China and Japan. There are also profiles of leading pottery and porcelain manufacturers; some background information on methods of ceramic construction and surface work; and a glossary of ceramic terminology.

While the depth of knowledge of the true expert requires years of experience in studying and handling antiques, *Collins need to know? Antique Marks* will provide you with the instant means to interpret the marks that are often crucial in assessing antique objects.

Nuremberg faïence jug, early 18th century

1 Precious metals

Precious metals are those materials favoured by craftsmen for making objects of beauty: gold, silver and in recent times platinum. The objects made in Europe were and are under the control of each country's government. Marks were struck on some part of the object to identify its date of manufacture, the place of origin and its maker. This section contains British hallmarks from the 16th century, location marks of government assay offices and a selection of British craftsmen's marks.

Hallmarks on silver, gold and platinum

Silver and gold are prized for their useful and attractive properties. Gold was one of the first metals to be discovered. Being soft and easy to work, colourful, bright and resistant to corrosion, it was ideal for jewellery and other decorative objects.

must know

The high value of these three metals makes it essential to have legally enforced standards of purity. The craft of the silversmith has been regulated by Parliamentary Acts and Royal Ordinances since the late 12th century.

Its scarcity ensured that its value remained high. Silver is harder and less scarce than gold, and more widely used in everyday life. Both have been mined in modest quantities in Britain since Roman times.

Platinum was unknown in Europe until 1600. It only became available commercially in the 19th century, and has been regulated in Britain since 1975. It is mainly used for jewellery.

Since 1 January 1975, a simplified scheme of hallmarks has been in use for British silver, gold and platinum, as directed by the 1973 Hallmarking Act.

Pre-1975 hallmarks and what they mean

Under British regulations, any object made of silver or gold is stamped with various 'hallmarks' to show when it was made, by whom, where it was made or tested for purity, and most importantly, how pure it is. The term 'hallmark' is derived from Goldsmiths' Hall, the guild hall of the London Goldsmiths' Company, the body that oversaw the first assay marks in Britain. In 1300, the sterling standard was established at 925 parts of silver per 1000. No object could leave the craftsman's hands until it had been assayed (tested) and marked with a punch depicting a leopard's head. Other assay offices were set up in the English provinces, in Scotland and Ireland, and all but the smallest had their own mark of origin.

Marks of origin on British silver to 1974

The mark of origin identifies the town or city where an item was assayed. Since 1300, London has used the leopard's head (**1**). An exception is the period 1697–1720, when the 'lion's head erased' (**2**) was used, when the Britannia standard replaced the Sterling standard for English silver. At Edinburgh, the earliest Scottish assay office, the mark of origin has always been a three-towered castle (**3**). Dublin has used a crowned harp (**4**) since the mid-17th century. Birmingham has long used an anchor (**5**), and Sheffield used a crown (**6**) for many years. More marks of origin are shown later in the chapter.

Sample marks of origin

1 2 3 4 5 6

Makers' marks

Since 1363, silversmiths have had to stamp their work with a registered mark. At first the custom was to use a rebus (for example, a picture of a fox for a silversmith whose surname was Fox) and initials combined in one mark. From 1697, makers had to use the first two letters of their surnames (**a**, **b** overleaf), but from 1720 initials again became the norm (**c**, **d**), sometimes with a symbol added (**e**, **f**).

In Scotland before about 1700, makers commonly used a monogram (**g**, **h**), later replaced by plain initials (**i**). Some used their full surname (**j**). In the case of factories or firms (**k**), the maker's mark is often called the 'sponsor's mark'.

must know

From 1478, a 'date mark' was required to be struck, a letter of the alphabet that signified the year in which the piece was assayed. This made it possible to trace the 'Keeper of the Touch' who had assayed a piece, in case of disputes as to purity. It now allows us to determine an accurate date for any piece of British plate.

A 'duty mark' depicting the head of the current monarch is found on plate assayed between 1784 and 1890, as proof that a tax on silver goods had been paid. The duty mark should not be confused with later commemorative stamps, which mark special occasions such as coronations and jubilees.

Sample makers' marks

a Thomas Sutton, London 1711
b John Farnell, London 1714
c William Woodward, London 1741
d Mathew Boulton, Birmingham 1790
e John Tuite, London 1739
f Thomas Morse, London 1720
g James Sympsone, Edinburgh 1687
h Robert Brook, Glasgow 1673
i Francis Howden, Edinburgh 1781
j Dougal Ged, Edinburgh 1734
k Lothian and Robertson, Edinburgh 1746

a 

b 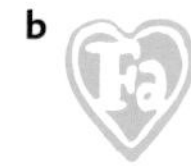
c 
d 

e 
f 

g 
h 
i 

j 

k 

Date letters to 1974

Date letters were introduced in England from 1478, in Scotland (Edinburgh) from 1681, and in Ireland (Dublin) from 1638, indicating the year when an item was assayed. The letters changed annually in a regular cycle. Different assay offices have used different cycles, lasting from 19 to 26 years, omitting various letters of the alphabet. 'I' was often used for 'J'. Each new cycle was given a new style of lettering and shape of shield, to distinguish one cycle from another.

Sample date letters

1 London 1561
2 London 1936
3 Birmingham 1891
4 Chester 1742
5 Dublin 1662
6 Edinburgh 1968

1 
2 

3 
4 
5 
6 

Standard marks to 1974

In England before 1544, the sterling silver standard of 92.5 per cent purity was vouched for by the leopard's head mark (**a**). In 1544, Henry VIII debased the coinage to only one third silver, and so a specific 'standard mark' showing a lion passant (**b**) was introduced for items that met the sterling standard. In 1697, the sterling standard was replaced by the Britannia standard of 95.84 per cent purity, to stop the melting down of coins for plate. The Britannia figure (**c**) replaced the lion passant as the standard mark, and the lion's head erased (**d**) replaced the leopard's head as the mark of origin.

Sample standard marks

a  b  c  d 

Duty marks 1784–1890

Between 1784 and 1890 a duty was imposed on most silver in Britain. An extra mark depicting the head of the current monarch was struck to show that tax had been paid. (In Dublin the duty was imposed only from 1807 and in Glasgow from 1819.) Silversmiths had many tricks to avoid paying duty.

1  2  3  4 

Duty marks

1 George III (1760–1820)
2 George IV (1820–1830)
3 William IV (1830–1837)
4 Victoria (1837–1901)

Commemorative marks

Special marks may be added to mark notable occasions. A mark with the heads of King George V and Queen Mary (**1**) was used for their Silver Jubilee in 1935. The coronation of Elizabeth II in 1953 was commemorated with a mark of the Queen's head (**2**). A similar mark (**3**) was used again to mark her Silver Jubilee in 1977, and a new mark (**4**) for her Golden Jubilee in 2002. Dublin, Birmingham and Sheffield assay offices have also used special marks to commemorate particular occasions.

1  2  3  4 

Marks on foreign silver to 1974

From 1867, a letter F (**a**, overleaf) was stamped on plate imported into Britain. From 1904, the value of the sterling (**b**) and Britannia (**c**) standards was marked as appropriate. Each assay office had a special mark of origin, in an oval shield.

a 

b 

c 

THE HALLMARKING ACT OF 1973

The Act governing hallmarks at all British assay offices came into force on 1 January 1975. Silver items of more than 7.8 grams must be hallmarked (gold items above 1 gram, platinum above 0.5 gram). There are four hallmarks: the registered maker's or sponsor's mark, the standard mark, the mark of origin, and the date letter.

Sample modern silver hallmarks
1 Maker's mark
2 Standard mark
3 Mark of origin
4 Date letter

1 

2 
3 
4 

Standard marks from 1975

On sterling silver, the English assay offices still use the lion passant (**a**), and the Edinburgh office in Scotland uses the lion rampant (**b**). All silver that meets the Britannia standard (**c**) receives that mark.

a 
b 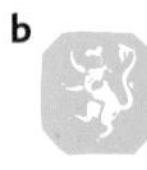
c  

Marks of origin from 1975

Since 1975, London has used a leopard's head (**1**), Birmingham its anchor (**2**) and Edinburgh its three-towered castle (**3**). Sheffield has adopted a York rose (**4**) to replace the crown, avoiding confusion with a similar mark on gold.

1 
2 
3 
4  

Date letters from 1975

The date letter now changes on 1 January, and is used by all four British assay offices.

Imported foreign silver from 1975

The 1973 Act also controls the marking of imported silver. The standard mark is the millesimal value in an oval shield (**a**, **b**). The four marks of origin are each contained in an oval shield (**c**–**f**).

a Sterling

b Britannia

c London

d Birmingham

e Sheffield

f Edinburgh

Convention marks

New regulations came into effect in the United Kingdom on 1 January 1999 implementing the judgement of The European Court of Justice that no member state of the European Union may require new hallmarks to be attached to properly hallmarked articles imported from other member states. All articles made from precious metals in the United Kingdom now have a standard metal fineness (purity) mark known as a common control mark (see right). The number gives the minimum quantity of the precious metal in the article in millesimals. The shape of the control mark indicates the type of precious metal.

The British Hallmarking Council

A body called the British Hallmarking Council was established under the 1973 Act, and became operative in 1975. The council coordinates the activities of the four assay offices, without hindering their independence. Its main responsibility is to ensure that adequate assaying facilities are available in the UK, and to see that laws relating to assaying are adhered to.

Common control marks

Gold

9 carat (37.5%)

14 carat (58.5%)

18 carat (75.0%)

22 carat (91.6%)

(99.0%)

(99.9%)

Silver

(80.0%)

sterling (92.5%)

Britannia (95.8%)

(99.9%)

Platinum

(85.0%)

(90.0%)

(95.0%)

(99.9%)

Sponsor's or maker's mark

Metal and fineness (purity) mark*

Assay office mark

London

Birmingham

Sheffield

Edinburgh

***This particular hallmark guarantees that the purity of the metal (whether silver, gold or platinum) is at least as great as that indicated by the Fineness Number.**

CURRENT UK HALLMARKS FOR SILVER

Compulsory marks since 1 January 1999

Following a new Act there are now three symbols that must appear on every UK hallmark:

A sponsor's or maker's mark

This mark indicates the maker and, in Britain, consists of at least two letters within a shield. No two marks are the same.

A metal and fineness mark

This mark indicates the precious metal content of the article; it also confirms that it is not less than the indicated fineness, or purity. Finenesses have been indicated by a millesimal number since 1999; this number is contained within a shield that depicts the precious metal.

An assay office mark

This mark indicates the particular British assay office (London, Birmingham, Sheffield or Edinburgh) at which the particular article was tested and marked.

Hallmarks on gold

Gold marks are much the same as silver marks. A set of gold hallmarks usually consists of four: a mark of origin, a standard mark, a date letter and a maker's mark. Duty marks and commemorative marks are also found at certain periods, just as on silver. Many changes have occurred over the years, most notably with the 1973 Hallmarking Act, which standardised hallmarking at all British assay offices.

Carat numbers

The carat number is the traditional measurement of purity for gold. One carat is equal to one twenty-fourth of the weight of an object. Thus a 22 carat object contains 22 parts gold and two parts alloy. A 9 carat object contains nine parts gold and 15 parts alloy.

Standard marks on British gold

Before 1363, a crowned leopard's head (see table opposite) denoted the gold standard of 19⅕ carat, and would be found near the mark of origin on an object. From 1363 onwards, the maker's mark was added to these marks. In 1477 the standard was reduced to 18 carat, but was denoted by the same mark (**1**). In 1478 date letters were first added, as on silver. 1544 saw the first change in the standard mark, to the lion passant (**2**). In 1575 the standard was increased to 22 carat, but using the same mark. In 1798 the 18 carat standard was reintroduced as an alternative, with new marks of a crown and a figure 18 (**3**). The 22 carat standard mark remained the lion passant. From 1844 the lion passant mark was replaced as the standard mark for 22 carat gold by a crown and the figure 22 (**4**). In 1854 three additional lower standards of 15 (**5**), 12 (**6**) and 9 (**7**) carat were introduced, with their standard marks as shown. This was the first time that millesimal numbers (giving the parts of gold per thousand) were used. The 15 and 12 carat standards were replaced in 1932 by 14 carat (**8**), along with a new mark for 9 carat (**9**). In Scotland up to 31 December 1974, the thistle was used (instead of the crown used in England), with the numbers 18 (**10**) or 22 (**11**) for the 18 or 22 carat gold standards respectively.

1 
19⅕ carat c1300–1476
18 carat 1477–1544

2
18 carat 1544–74
22 carat 1575–1843

3
18 carat 1798–1974

4 
22 carat 1844–1974

5 
15 carat 1854–1931

6 
12 carat 1854–1931

7 
9 carat 1854–1931

8 
14 carat 1932–74

9 
9 carat 1932–74

Scotland

10  
18 carat Edinburgh 1759–1974

11  
22 carat Glasgow 1914–74

  22 carat

  18 carat

  14 carat

  9 carat

a  22 carat 1637–1784

b   22 carat 1784–today

c   20 carat 1784–today

d 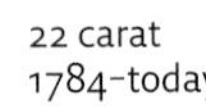   18 carat 1784–today

e   14 carat 1935–today

f   9 carat 1854–today

Hallmarking Act 1973

From 1 January 1975, gold standard marks were made the same at all English and Scottish assay offices, becoming a crown mark next to the millesimal value.

Standard marks on Irish gold

At Dublin from 1637 to 1784, the same marks as used for silver were used for gold, with the standard being set at 22 carat and the mark a crowned harp (**a**). From 1784 there were three standards of 22 (**b**), 20 (**c**) and 18 (**d**) carat, each using a symbol and number as its mark, as shown. From 1854 three additional lower standards were introduced, of 15 carat (stamped '15' and '.625'), 12 carat (stamped '12' and '.5') and 9 carat (**f**). In 1935 the 15 and 12 carat standards were replaced with 14 carat (**e**), giving the five standards of 22, 20 (rare), 18, 14 and 9 carat found today.

Marks of origin on British and Irish gold

The marks of origin placed on gold by the various assay offices have generally been the same as those placed on silver. However, Birmingham and Dublin have always turned their usual mark on its side in the case of gold. When Sheffield first assayed gold in 1904, it was already using a crown as its town mark for silver. So, to avoid confusion with the crown used as the British standard mark for gold, Sheffield adopted a rose as its town mark on gold. Since 1975 it has used the same York rose on silver and gold alike.

Other marks

Date letters, makers' marks, commemorative marks and duty marks have always been applied to gold just as to silver. Convention marks for gold also follow the same system as on silver (see page 15).

Marks of origin on British and Irish gold

IMPORTED GOLD

Standard marks on imported gold

From 1904 to 1974, combined carat and millesimal marks were used. Since 1975 simple millesimal marks have been used.

Carat	1904-32	1932-74	From 1974
22	22 ·916	22 ·916	916
18	18 ·75	18 ·750	750
15	15 ·625	—	—
14	—	14 ·585	585
12	12 ·5	—	—
9	9 ·375	9 ·375	375

Marks of origin on imported gold

From 1876 to 1904, each assay office used its usual mark of origin for gold plus a letter F in an oval or rectangle. From 1904 each office adopted a special mark (right).

All offices (1876–1904)

Birmingham (1904–today)

Chester (1904–62)

Dublin (1904–06)

Dublin (1906–today)

Edinburgh (1904–today)

Glasgow (1904–06)

Glasgow (1906–64)

London (1904–06)

London (1906–today)

Sheffield (1904–1906)

Sheffield (1906–today)

CURRENT UK HALLMARKS FOR GOLD

Compulsory marks

Amendments to the Hallmarking Act, effective from 1 January 1999, changed the way in which articles made of precious metal are hallmarked. There are now three symbols that are compulsory on every UK hallmark.

A sponsor's or maker's mark

This mark indicates the maker of the article and, in Britain, consists of at least two letters within a shield. No two marks are the same.

A metal and fineness mark

This mark indicates the precious metal content of the article; it also confirms that it is not less than the indicated fineness, or purity. Finenesses have been indicated by a millesimal number since 1999; a surrounding shield indicates the precious metal.

An assay office mark

This mark indicates the particular British assay office (London, Birmingham, Sheffield or Edinburgh) at which the article was tested and marked.

Sponsor's or maker's mark

Metal and fineness (purity) mark*

Assay office mark

London

Birmingham

Sheffield

Edinburgh

***This hallmark guarantees that the purity of the metal (whether silver, gold or platinum) is at least as great as that indicated by the Fineness Number.**

Hallmarks on platinum

Most platinum comes from Latin America. The metal was unknown in Europe before 1600, and it was not until the 19th century that it was worked into jewellery. In Britain there was no legal requirement to mark platinum until 1975, when the Hallmarking Act 1973 came into force. There is now a single standard for platinum, set at 950 parts per thousand, and all items weighing more than 0.5 grams must be marked.

As with silver and gold, a set of hallmarks for British platinum consists of four elements: a maker's mark, the standard mark, a mark of origin and a date letter. The platinum standard mark is an orb with a cross on top.

Imported platinum also bears four marks, but the standard mark is the figure 950, and the mark of origin used by each assay office has the same symbol as placed on imported silver or gold, but contained in a distinctive roof-shaped shield in the case of platinum.

British

	Origin	Standard
London		
Birmingham		
Sheffield		
Edinburgh		

Imported

	Origin	Standard
London		950
Birminghan		950
Sheffield		950
Edinburgh	X	950

CURRENT UK HALLMARKS FOR PLATINUM

Compulsory marks

The Hallmarking Act, effective from 1 January 1999, changed the way in which articles made of precious metal are hallmarked. There are now three compulsory symbols that must appear on every UK hallmark.

A sponsor's or maker's mark

This mark indicates the maker of the article and, in Britain, consists of at least two letters within a shield. No two marks are the same.

Sponsor's or maker's mark

Metal and fineness (purity) mark*

Assay office mark

London

Birmingham

Sheffield

Edinburgh

***This particular hallmark guarantees that the purity of the metal (whether silver, gold or platinum) is at least as great as that indicated by the Fineness Number.**

A metal and fineness mark

This mark indicates the precious metal content of the article; it also confirms that it is not less than the indicated fineness, or purity. Finenesses have been indicated by a millesimal number since 1999; a surrounding shield indicates the precious metal.

An assay office mark

This mark indicates the particular British assay office (London, Birmingham, Sheffield or Edinburgh) at which the particular article was tested and marked.

CURRENT INTERNATIONAL HALLMARKS

Convention marks

Since 1972, the UK has been a signatory to the International Convention on Hallmarks. UK assay offices can therefore strike the Convention hallmark, which will be recognised by all member countries. Convention hallmarks from other member countries are also legally recognised in the UK, and articles bearing such hallmarks do not have to be re-marked in the UK.

The following four illustrations are examples of Convention hallmarks:

Sponsor's or maker's mark

Common control mark

Fineness (purity) mark

Assay office mark

The assay office marks of the member countries of the International Convention on Hallmarks are shown below. The design in the form of a shield that appears around the mark sometimes varies according to whether the article is gold, silver or platinum.

Although the common control mark is crucial, the other three marks must also be present on the article.

Assay office mark

1 

2 

3 

4 

5 

6 

7 

8 

9 

10 

11 

12 

13 

14 

1 Austria
2 Czech Republic
3 Denmark
4 Finland
5 Ireland
6 Netherlands
7 Norway
8 Portugal
9 Sweden
10 Switzerland

United Kingdom
11 London
12 Birmingham
13 Sheffield
14 Edinburgh

Sponsor's or maker's mark

Common control mark

Gold **Silver** **Platinum**

Metal and fineness (purity) mark*

Gold	Silver	Platinum
375	800	950
585	925	
750		

***This hallmark guarantees that the purity of the precious metal is at least as great as that indicated by the Fineness Number.**

must know

HOW TO READ HALLMARKS

- ▷ Study the mark of origin to find out where the piece was assayed. (If there is no assay office's mark, the piece probably comes from London.)
- ▷ Find the relevant city's section in the tables of hallmarks, look at the date letter and see if it is a capital or small letter; check which kind of script it is in; and note the shape of the shield containing it.
- ▷ Compare these with the city's tables. When you find an exact match for your hallmark you can be confident about its date.
- ▷ With the place and date of origin known, look up the maker's or sponsor's mark and find out the name of the craftsman or company.
- ▷ Other marks will indicate if the piece is sterling or Britannia silver, if duty was paid on it, and whether it was made in a coronation or jubilee year.

READING THE HALLMARK CHARTS IN THIS BOOK

The charts on the pages that follow show the hallmarks associated with each of the towns or cities that have had important assay offices, presented in the order in which the assay offices were established. Within each section, all the variations in the design of that city's mark of origin (**b**) and the standard marks (**c** and sometimes **d**) are illustrated, and these are followed by any duty marks or commemorative marks (**e**) and by the date letters (**f**). Unusual marks are fully explained in special feature panels (**a**). Makers' marks are shown separately in lists at the end of each city's section.

For gold, the marks of origin are the same as for silver, except in the cases of Birmingham and Dublin (see pages 135–6). Date letters are the same for gold and platinum as they are for silver.

Note that the hallmark charts apply primarily to silver (as they show the standard marks for silver), but that the same date letters apply equally to British gold.

Here is a sample of a set of marks which you may be looking for (although they may not appear in this order):

b  **c**  **e**  **f** 

In the charts they would be shown as follows:

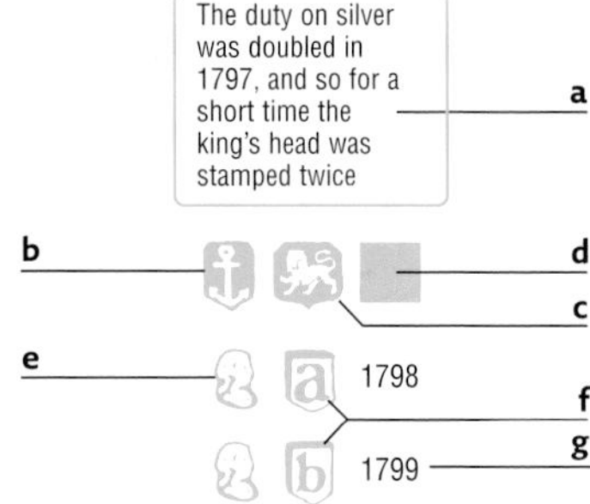

a Text box for unusual markings
b Mark of origin
c Standard mark
d Possible second standard mark
e Duty or commemorative mark
f Date letter mark
g Text showing year

British assay offices: London

The Goldsmiths' Company in London was the first in England authorised to assay and mark gold and silver, granted a Royal Charter in 1327. In terms of quantity, quality and variety, London remains the premier assay office in Britain today.

Its mark is a leopard's head. The precise shape has varied over the years. From 1697 until 1720 the leopard's head was replaced by the lion's head erased, and the Britannia mark. From 1784 until 1890 the sovereign's head duty mark was used.

From 1478 to 1974 London used a 20-letter sequence that changed in May; since 1975 it has changed on 1 January.

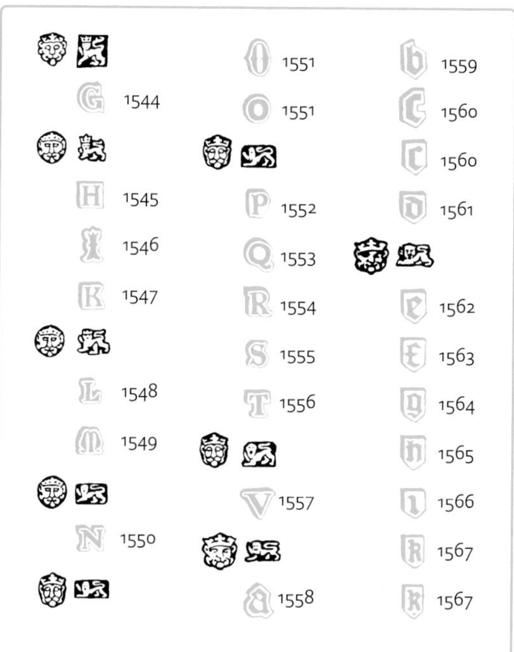

must know

London gold and silver dated between 1544 and 1555 bears the oldest date marks in Britain.

Marks from this period date from the reigns of Henry VIII and two of his three children, Edward VI and Mary (1509–58).

must know

Do not regard old hallmarks as definitive indicators of date, as they can be worn to illegibility, faked, or even let-in from other pieces.

London date marks run from A to U, omitting J; the 20-letter sequence is then repeated.

All the marks during this period were produced during the reign of Elizabeth I (1558–1603).

In 1603 James VI of Scotland became King of England, uniting the crowns of the two countries for the first time.

1568	1578	1590
1569	1579	1591
1570	1580	
1571	1581	1592
1572	1582	1593
1573	1583	1594
1574	1584	1595
1575	1585	1596
1575	1586	1597
1576	1587	
1577	1588	1598
	1589	1599

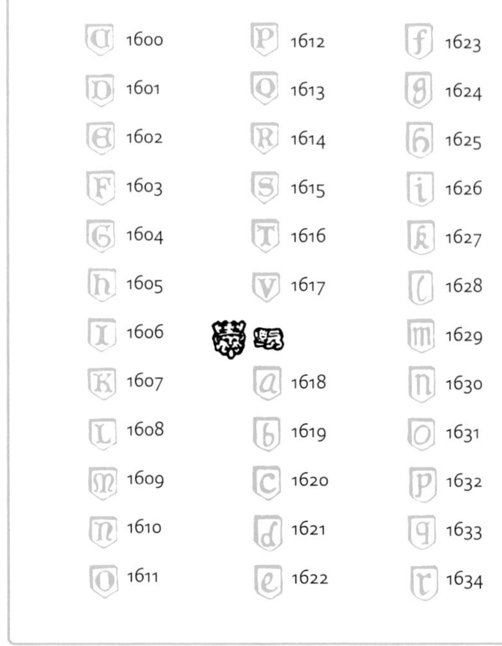

1635	1646	1657
1636		
1637	1647	1658
	1648	1659
1638	1649	1660
1639	1650	1661
1640	1651	1662
1641	1652	1663
1642	1653	1664
1643	1654	1665
1644	1655	1666
1645	1656	1667

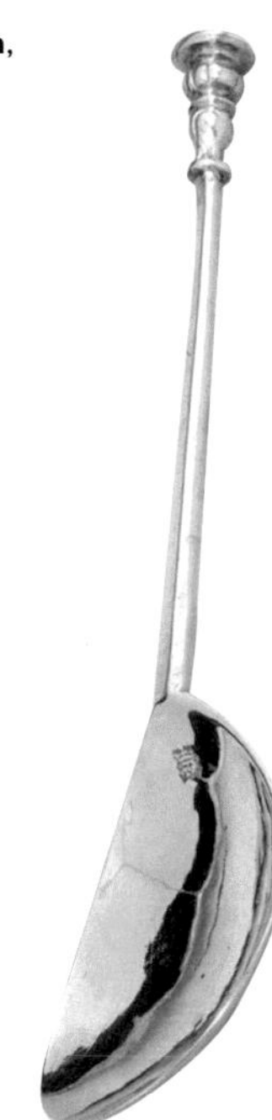

Seal top spoon, c. 1630s

		1688
1668	1678	1689
1669	1679	1690
1670		1691
1671	1680	1692
1672	1681	1693
1672	1682	1694
1673	1683	1695
1674	1684	1696–97
1675	1685	
1676	1686	1697
1677	1687	1697

must know

Silverware of this period is rather light in weight as the metal was in short supply.

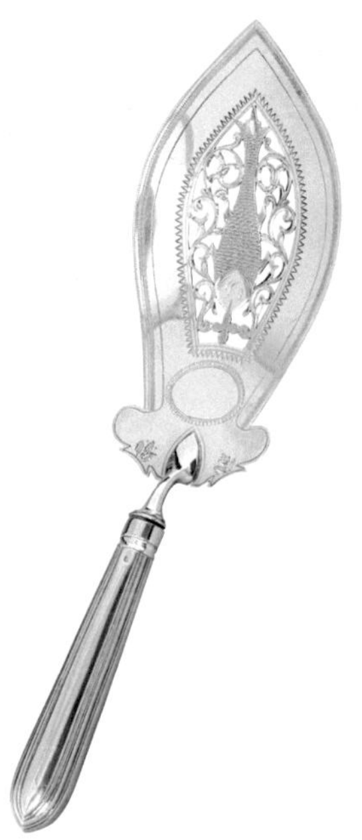

Silver-handled fishslice, 1747

must know

Silver from this period is heavier than previously and fairly plain in form and decoration.

From 1714 to 1830, four kings called George governed Britain: this period is therefore known as the Georgian period.

I 1724
K 1725
L 1726
M 1727
N 1728
O 1729
P 1730
Q 1731
R 1732
S 1733
T 1734
V 1735
a 1736
b 1737
c 1738
d 1739
d 1739
e 1740
f 1741
g 1742
h 1743
i 1744
k 1745
l 1746
m 1747
n 1748
o 1749
p 1750
q 1751
r 1752
f 1753

t 1754
u 1755
A 1756
B 1757
C 1758
D 1759
E 1760
F 1761
G 1762
H 1763
I 1764
k 1765
L 1766
M 1767
N 1768
O 1769
P 1770
Q 1771
R 1772
S 1773
T 1774
T 1774
U 1775

Two shield shapes for standard mark found, 1776-1795

From 1776 to 1875, a shield without a point was used for some small articles

a 1776
b 1777
c 1778
d 1779

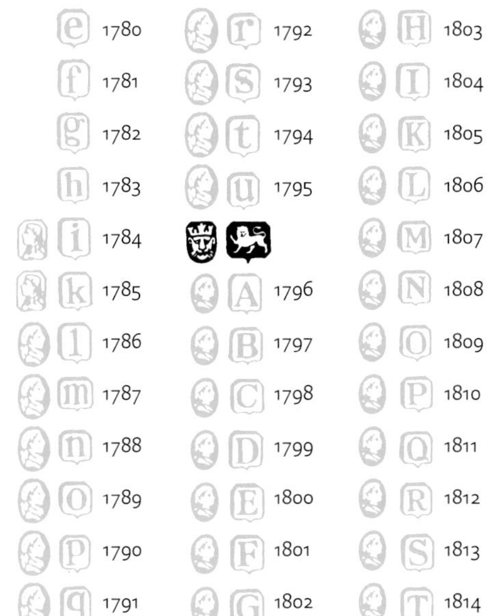

must know

Increasing prosperity during the reign of George II (1727–60) leads to a greater degree of ornamentation on gold and silverware that lasts until the introduction of neoclassical designs in the late 18th century.

Be careful when buying single items that may originally have been part of a set or pair, as the price should reflect this.

Hester Bateman silver sugar basket, 1789

must know

An 1844 act of parliament makes it an offence to make unhallmarked additions to a piece or to alter its purpose, for example turning a christening mug into a cream jug.

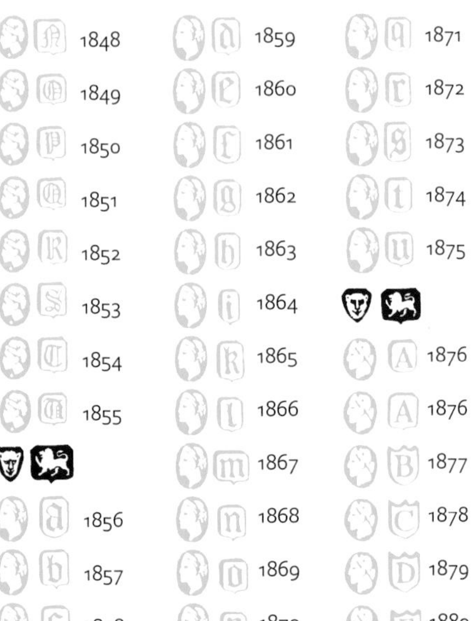

Cigarette lighter, 1871

Victorian "heart" mirror, 1899

t 1914
u 1915
a 1916
b 1917
c 1918
d 1919
e 1920
f 1921
g 1922
h 1923
i 1924
k 1925
l 1926
m 1927
n 1928
o 1929
p 1930
q 1931
r 1932
s 1933
t 1934
u 1935
A 1936
B 1937
C 1938
D 1939
E 1940
F 1941
G 1942
H 1943
I 1944
K 1945
L 1946

must know

Gold and silver production in this period is twice disrupted by the world wars.

The main style between the wars (1918–39) is Art Deco, with its geometric forms and undecorated surfaces.

Wine taster, 1960, top and side view

Letter	Year	Letter	Year	Letter	Year
M	1947	a	1956	n	1968
N	1948	b	1957	o	1969
O	1949	c	1958	p	1970
P	1950	d	1959	q	1971
Q	1951	e	1960	r	1972
R	1952	f	1961	s	1973
S	1953	g	1962	t	1974
T	1954	h	1963		
U	1955	i	1964		
		k	1965		
		l	1966		
		m	1967	A	1975

New letter sequence commenced on 1 January 1975, in accordance with the Hallmarking Act passed in 1973

must know

As a result of the Hallmarking Act of 1975, the letter sequence now runs from A-Z, omitting J.

The Queen's head mark in 1977 commemorates her Silver Jubilee.

Letter	Year	Letter	Year	Letter	Year
B	1976	M	1986	Y	1998
C	1977	N	1987	Z	1999
D	1978	O	1988	a	2000
E	1979	P	1989	b	2001
F	1980	Q	1990	c	2002
G	1981	R	1991	d	2003
H	1982	S	1992	e	2004
I	1983	T	1993	f	2005
K	1984	U	1994	g	2006
L	1985	V	1995	h	2007
		W	1996	i	2008
		X	1997	j	2009

London makers' marks (A–M)

ABS	Adey B Savory
AF **SG**	Andrew Fogelberg & Stephen Gilbert
AS	Thomas Ash
BC	Benjamin Cooper
BS	Benjamin Smith
BS **BS**	Benjamin Smith & Son
Bu/BU	Thomas Burridge
CF	Charles Fox or Crispin Fuller
CK	Charles F Kandler (star below)
CO	Augustin Courtauld (fleur-de-lys above)
CR	Charles Rawlins
CR **DR**	Christian & David Reid
CR **GS**	Charles Reilly & George Storer
CR **WS**	Charles Rawlins & William Summers
DH	David Hennell
DM	Dorothy Mills
DPW	Dobson, Prior & Williams
DS **BS**	Digby Scott & Benjamin Smith
DS **RS**	Daniel Smith & Robert Sharp
EC	Ebenezer Coker
EF	Edward Feline
ET	Elizabeth Tuite
EW	Edward Wigan
EY	Edward Yorke
FC	Francis Crump
FO	Thomas Folkingham
GA	George Adams
GS	George Smith
GS **WF**	George Smith & William Fearn
GW	George Wintle
HA	Pierre Harache (crown above)
HB	Hester Bateman
HC	Henry Chawner
HC **IE**	Henry Chawner & John Emes
HN	Hannah Northcote
IB	James Bult
IC	John Carter
IG	John Gould
IH	John Hyatt
IL **HL**	John & Henry Lias
IL **HL** **CL**	John, Henry & Charles Lias
IP	John Pollock
IS	John Swift or John Scholfield
IW **IT**	John Walcelon & John Taylor
JA	Joseph Angell
JA **JA**	J & J Aldous
JC	John Cafe
JE	John Emes
JL	John Lias
LA	Paul de Lamerie (crown and star above)
LO	Nathaniel Lock
LP	Lewis Pantin
MC	Mary Chawner
ME	Louis Mettayer
MP	Mary Pantin
MS	Mary Sumner
MS **ES**	Mary & Elizabeth Sumner

must know

Among the many London silversmiths, the most prized and collected are Andrew Fogelberg, Benjamin Smith, Charles Fox, David and Samuel Hennell, George Adams, Hester Bateman, John Café, Anthony Nelme, Pierre Platel, Paul de Lamerie, Paul Storr, Rebecca Emes, Robert Garrard, Thomas Hemming and William Eley.

Hester Bateman senior, script mark HB entered at the Goldsmiths' Hall in 1761.

Silversmithing is by no means an exclusively male occupation, as proved by Hester Bateman, one of the most famous London silversmiths.

London makers' marks (N–W)

Ne	Anthony Nelme
NS	Nicholas Sprimont
PB **AB**	Peter & Anne Bateman
PB **AB** **WB**	Peter, Anne & William Bateman
PB **IB**	Peter & Jonathan Bateman
PL	Pierre Platel
PL	Paul de Lamerie (crown and star above, fleur-de-lys below)
PS	Paul Storr
Py	Benjamin Pyne (rose and crown above)
RC	Richard Crossley
RC **GS**	Richard Crossley & George Smith
R **DH** **H**	Robert & David Hennell
RE **EB**	Rebecca Emes & Edward Barnard
RE **WE**	Rebecca & William Emes
RG	Robert Garrard
RH	Robert Hennell
RH **DH**	Robert & David Hennell
RH **DH** **SH**	Robert, David & Samuel Hennell
RH **SH**	Robert & Samuel Hennell
RM **RC**	Robert Makepeace & Richard Carter
RM **TM**	Robert & Thomas Makepeace
Ro	Philip Rolles
RR	Richard Rugg or Robert Rutland
RS	Robert Swanson
SA	Stephen Adams
Sc	William Scarlett
SC **IC**	S & J Crespell
SG	Samuel Godbehere
SG **EW**	Samuel Godbehere & Edward Wigan
SL	Gabriel Sleath
SM	Samuel Meriton
Sp	Thomas Spackman
S **WI** **A**	Stephen Adams & William Jury
TH	Thomas Heming
TH **IC**	Thomas Hannam & John Crouch
T & W	Turner & Williams
TN	Thomas Northcote
TO	Thomas Oliphant
TP **ER**	Thomas Phipps & Edward Robinson
TP **ER** **JP**	Thomas Phipps, Edward Robinson & James Phipps
TP **IP**	Thomas & James Phipps
TR	Thomas Robins
T **WC** **C**	Thomas & William Chawner
WB	William Burwash
WC	William Cafe
WE	William Eaton or William Eley
WE **CE** **HE**	William, Charles & Henry Eley
WE **GP**	William Eley & George Pierrepont
WE **WF**	William Eley & William Fearn
WF	William Fearn
WF **PS**	William Frisbee & Paul Storr
WG	William Grundy
WI	David Willaume
WP	William Peaston or William Plummer
WRS	W R Smiley
WS	William Sumner or William Smiley
WT	William Tweedie
W **WP** **S**	William Shaw & William Priest

must know

The art of silversmithing is often handed down through generations of the same family, so it is important to identify the right family member's mark.

William Cafe

Edinburgh

An Incorporation of Goldsmiths existed from at least the 1490s and silver was assayed in Edinburgh from the 1500s. Edinburgh has long been known for ecclesiastical and domestic silverware.

The Edinburgh mark is a three-towered castle. Before 1681 the standard mark was the Deacon's mark, a monogram of the initials of the current Deacon. After 1681 it was the Assay Master's mark - again the office-holder's initials - replaced in 1759 by a thistle, and in 1975 by a lion rampant. From 1784 to 1890 the sovereign's head duty mark was in use.

In 1836 the Sterling standard was adopted and, in 1975, the standard British date letter sequence.

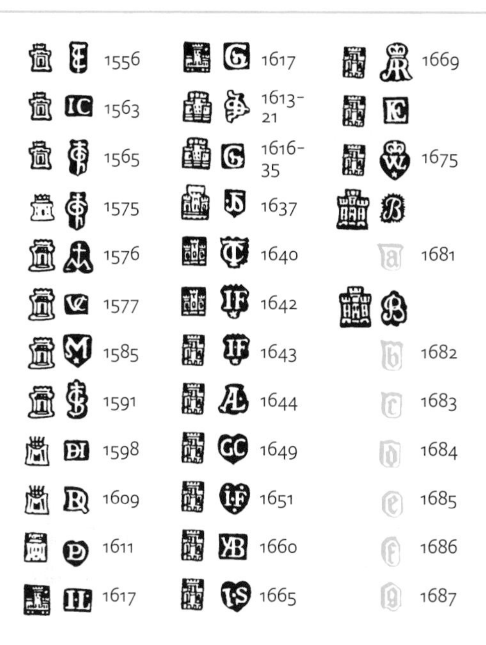

must know

The castle mark of origin and the deacon's mark changes yearly during this period, making dating easier if the hallmarks are worn.

must know

From 1681 onwards, the castle mark of origin and assay master's mark change less frequently, although individual year marks make dating simple.

Edinburgh generally uses a 25-letter dating system at this period, omitting the letter J.

In some years, such as 1719, 1725, and 1763, two date marks are used in one year.

1688
1689
1690
1691
1692
1693
1694
1695
1696
P
1697
P
1698
1699
1700
1701
P
1702
1703
1704
P
1705
1706
EP
1707
1708
1709
1710
1711
EP
1712
1713
EP
1714
1715
1716

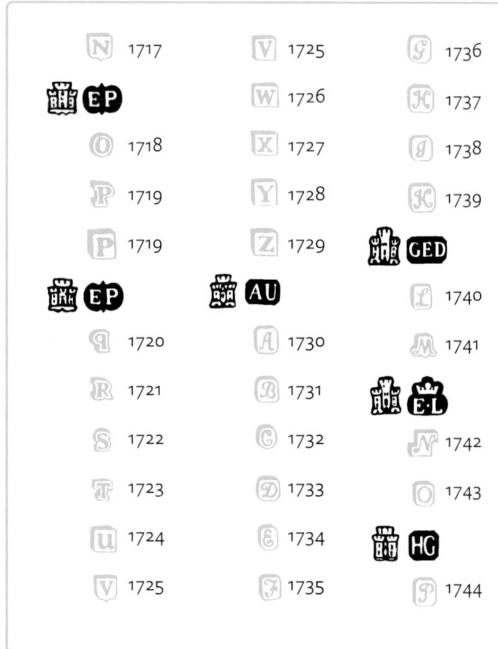

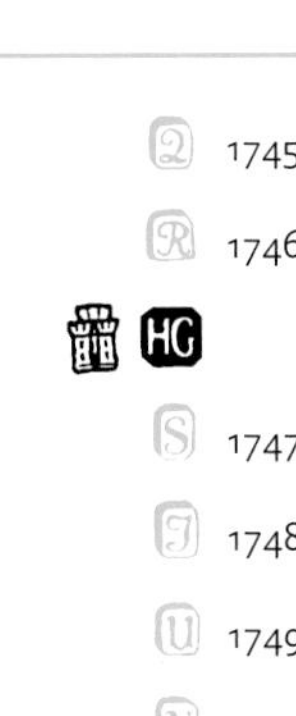

1745	1755	1764
1746	1756	1765
HG	1757	1766
1747	1758	1767
1748		1768
1749	1759	1769
1750	1760	1770
1751	1761	1771
1752	1762	These alternative town marks are found c. 1771
1753		
1754	1763	1772
HG	1763	1773

Drinking flask, 1782

1774	1785	1795
1775	1786–87	1796
1776	1788	
1777	1789	1797
1778	1789	1797
1779	1790	1798
	1791	
1780	1792	1799
1781	1793	1800
1782	1793	1801
1783	1794	
1784	1794	1802

Hanoverian pattern soup ladle, 1776

must know

During this period, construction of the New Town in Edinburgh finally finishes. It is one of the finest examples of neoclassical architecture in the world. The rich aristocracy and professional middle classes live here, all eager customers for Edinburgh gold and silver.

Wine goblet, 1807

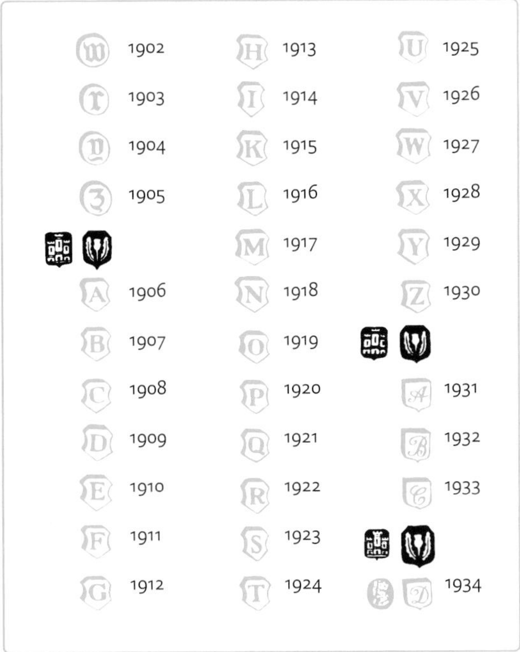

Letter	Year	Letter	Year	Letter	Year
L	1867	X	1879	i	1890
M	1868	Y	1880	k	1891
N	1869	Z	1881	l	1892
O	1870			m	1893
P	1871	a	1882	n	1894
Q	1872	b	1883	o	1895
R	1873	c	1884	p	1896
S	1874	d	1885	q	1897
T	1875	e	1886	r	1898
U	1876	f	1887	s	1899
V	1877	g	1888	t	1900
W	1878	h	1889	u	1901

Letter	Year	Letter	Year	Letter	Year
w	1902	H	1913	U	1925
x	1903	I	1914	V	1926
y	1904	K	1915	W	1927
z	1905	L	1916	X	1928
		M	1917	Y	1929
A	1906	N	1918	Z	1930
B	1907	O	1919		
C	1908	P	1920	*A*	1931
D	1909	Q	1921	*B*	1932
E	1910	R	1922	*C*	1933
F	1911	S	1923		
G	1912	T	1924	*D*	1934

must know

From 1836 onwards, Edinburgh adopts the sterling silver standard.

The Forth Railway Bridge opens in 1890, connecting Edinburgh by rail to Fife and the ports of the east coast, such as Dundee and Aberdeen.

The Scottish Nationalist Party is founded in 1928; its first MP is elected briefly in 1945.

must know

The annual Edinburgh Festival begins in 1947 and is now the largest arts festival in the world, encompassing music, opera, theatre, jazz, dance, television and a vibrant Festival Fringe of alternative events.

The Edinburgh Assay Office is still in use, along with London, Birmingham and Sheffield. Edinburgh continues to use the lion rampant and the three-towered castle.

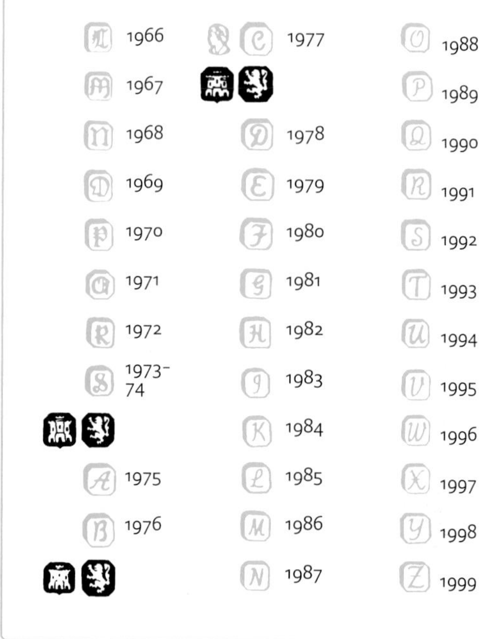

a	2000	d	2003	g	2006
b	2001	e	2004	h	2007
c	2002	f	2005	i	2008

Edinburgh makers' marks (A–W)

Mark	Maker	Mark	Maker
AE	Alexander Edmonstone	**JMc**	John McKay
AG	Alexander Gairdner	**JN**	James Nasmyth
AH	Alexander Henderson	**J & WM**	James & William Marshall
AK	Alexander Kincaid	**LO**	Lawrence Oliphant
AS	Alexander Spencer	**LU**	Leonard Urquhart
AZ	Alexander Zeigler	**MC**	Matthew Craw
CD	Charles Dixon	**M & C**	McKay & Chisholm
E & Co	Elder & Co	**M & F**	McKay & Fenwick
EL	Edward Lothian	**M & S**	Marshall & Sons
EO	Edward Oliphant	**MY**	Mungo Yorstoun
GC	George Christie	**PM**	Peter Mathie
GF	George Fenwick	**PR**	Patrick Robertson
G & K	Gilsland & Ker	**PS**	Peter Sutherland
GMH	George McHattie	**RB**	Robert Bowman
GS	George Scott	**RC**	Robert Clark
HB	Henry Beathume	**RG**	Robert Gordon
HG	Hugh Gordon	**RI**	Robert Inglis
ID	James Dempster	**RK**	Robert Ker
IG	John Gilsland	**WG**	William Ged
IK	James Ker	**W & PC**	William & Peter Cunningham
IR	James Rollo	**WR**	William Robertson
IW	John Walsh	**WS**	Walter Scott
IZ	John Zeigler	**WT & IT**	William & Jonathan Taylor
JD	James Douglas		
JM	Jonathan Millidge		

must know

Until 1603, Scotland is an independent country with its own king and parliament in Edinburgh. When Elizabeth I of England dies in 1603, James VI of Scotland moves south to become king of both countries, uniting the two crowns.

In 1707 the Scottish parliament votes for union with England, ending its parliamentary independence and giving the Scots a voice in the London parliament for the first time. From 1784 to 1890, the sovereign's head duty mark appears on Edinburgh silver, as it does for all the other assay offices.

In 1759 the Edinburgh Assay Office begins to use a thistle instead of an assay master's mark.

York

Silver was assayed in York from the mid-16th century. York silver, often Scandinavian in style, is generally of basic design for everyday use. From 1717 to 1776 the York Assay Office closed, and York silver was assayed at Newcastle. York Assay Office closed in 1856.

The York mark was initially a halved leopard's head conjoined with a halved fleur-de-lys in a round shield. In the late 17th century the halved leopard's head was replaced by a halved seeded rose. A new mark of five lions passant on a cross was introduced in 1751. Numerous marks were then used until 1784 when the sovereign's head mark was introduced.

must know

York has the third oldest series of date marks, after London and Edinburgh.

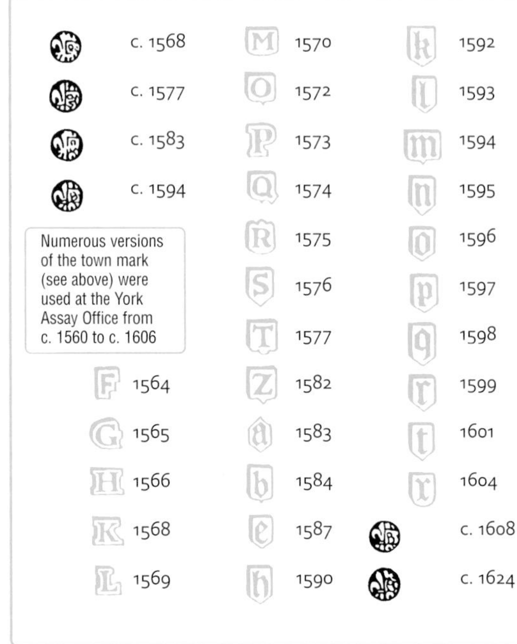

From 1607 to 1630, two versions of the town mark (see previous page) were used at the York Assay Office

1607
1608
1609
1610
1611
1612
1613
1614
1615

1616
1617
1618
1619
1620
1621
1622
1623
1624
1625
1626
1627

1628
1629
1630

From 1631 to 1656, two versions of the town mark (see below) were used at York Assay Office

1631
1632
1633
1634
1635

1636
1637
1638
1639
1641
1642
1643
1645
1649
1650
1651
1652

1653
1654
1655
1656

1657
1658
1659
1660
1661
1662
1663

1664
1665
1666
1667
1668
1669
1670
1671
1672
1673
1674
1675

must know

Objects in this period (1558 to 1618) are in the Elizabethan style which encompasses the reign of Elizabeth I and her father Henry VIII.

During the English civil wars (1642–49), Charles I establishes his court in this fiercely royal city. Royalist forces in the city are besieged unsuccessfully by parliamentary forces in April 1644 but three months later the royalists suffer a huge defeat at Marston Moor, six miles west of York.

must know

During this period, York begins to emerge as a social centre for Yorkshire's landed gentry.

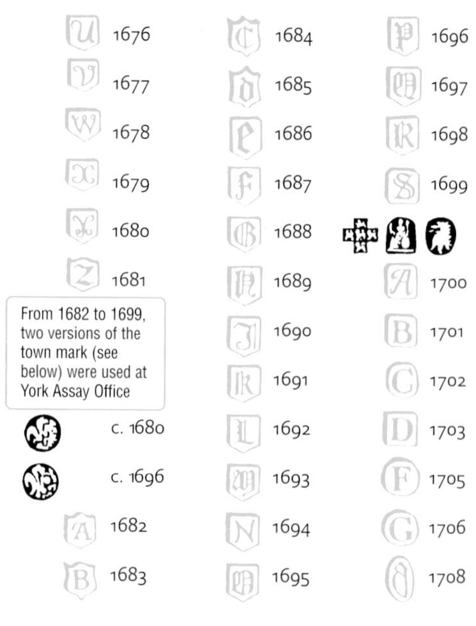

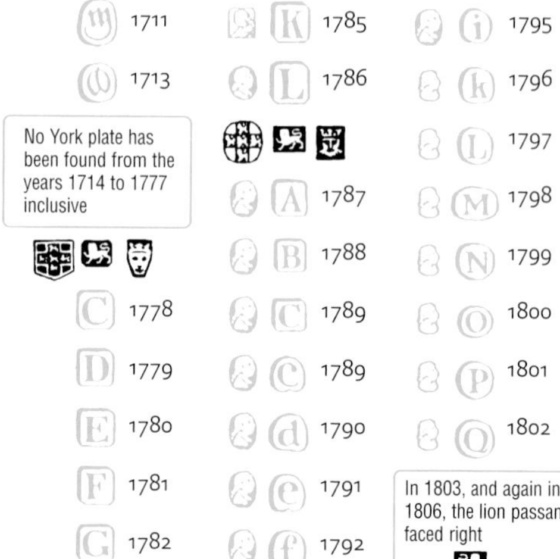

Horseracing ticket, 1754

1805
1806
1807
1808
1809
1810
1811
1812
1813
1814
1815
1816
1817
1818
1819
1820
1821
1822
1823
1824
1825
1826
1827
1828
1829
1830
1831
1832
1833
1834
1835
1836
1837
1838

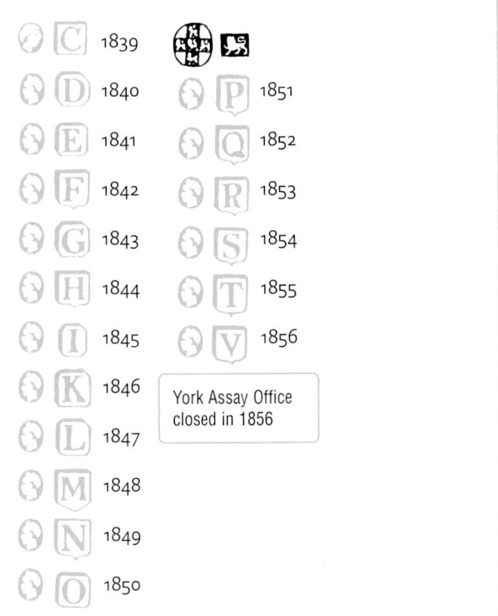

must know

From 1787 onwards, York adopts a 25-letter date sequence, omitting J.

The arrival of the railways during the 1830s brings great prosperity to York.

For the last six years of the York Assay Office's existence, the leopard's head is dropped from the city's hallmark.

York makers' marks (B–R)

BC & N	James Barber, George Cattle, William North
B & N	James Barber, William North
Bu	William Busfield
HP & C	John Hampston, John Prince, Robert Cattle
IH IP	John Hampston & John Prince
JB & Co	James Barber & Co.
JB GC WN	James Barber, George Cattle, William North
JB WN	James Barber, William North
JB WW	James Barber, William Whitwell
La	John Langwith
TM	Thomas Mangy
P & Co	John Prince, Robert Cattle
RC JB	Robert Cattle, James Barber

William Busfield

Hampton & Prince

James Barber & William North

Thomas Mangy

Thomas Mangy

Norwich

The earliest known Norwich silver marks date from the mid-16th century. The city is known principally for ecclesiastical and corporation plate.

The town mark was a lion passant surmounted by a castle. From the early 17th century a crowned seeded rose was also used, and variations of both marks appeared until 1701. After 1701 virtually no silver was assayed in Norwich.

Norwich used a 21-letter date sequence (A to V omitting J). The letter was changed each September. There are few recorded makers' marks from Norwich.

Letter	Date	Letter	Date	Letter	Date
A	1565		c. 1600	G	1630
B	1566		c. 1610	H	1631
C	1567		c. 1620	I	1632
D	1568			K	1633
E	1569			L	1634
F	1570			M	1635
G	1571	A	1624	N	1636
I	1573	B	1625	O	1637
K	1574	C	1626	P	1638
P	1579	D	1627	Q	1639
	c. 1620	E	1628	R	1640
	c. 1620	F	1629	S	1641

Several versions of the town marks shown below were used 1624–1643 (e.g. as above for c. 1620)

The Peterson cup, 1574

must know

Marks from this period are bound to be faint or worn, so they must be checked carefully to establish the correct date.

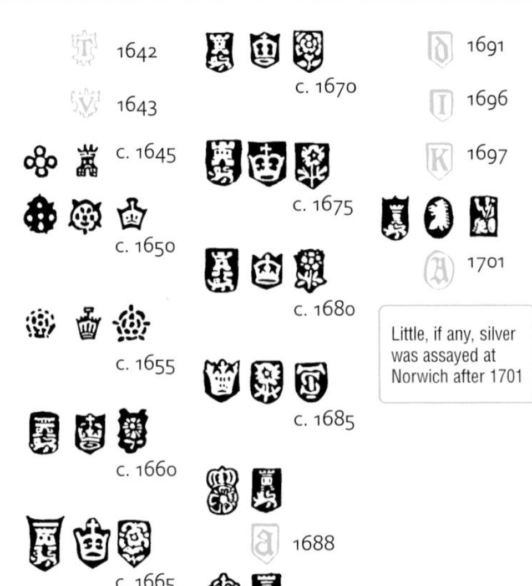

Norwich makers' marks (B–P)

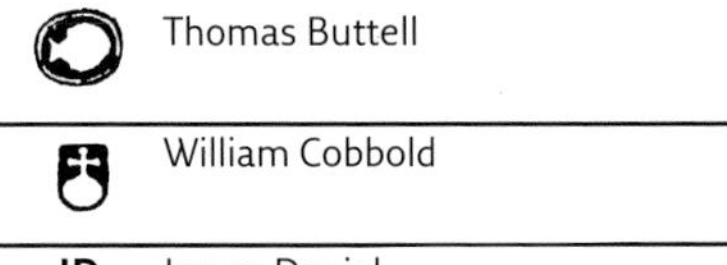

Mark	Maker	Mark	Maker
	Thomas Buttell	AH	Arthur Haselwood
	William Cobbold	EH	Elizabeth Haselwood
ID	James Daniel	TH	Thomas Havers
			Peter Peterson

Elizabeth Haselwood

Thomas Havers

James Daniel

Exeter

The earliest assay marks date from the mid-16th century. Exeter is known for a good standard of ecclesiastical and domestic silver, but small items were rarely made.

The mark of origin was a round shield containing the letter X surmounted by a crown, replaced after 1701 by a three-towered castle. From 1701 to 1720 the Britannia mark and the lion's head erased were in use together. After 1721 these were replaced with the leopard's head (omitted from 1777) and the lion passant in square shields. The sovereign's head duty mark was in use from 1784 to 1882.

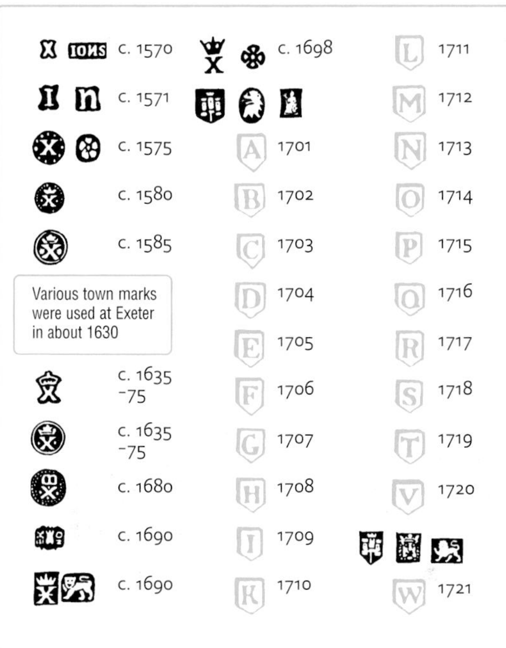

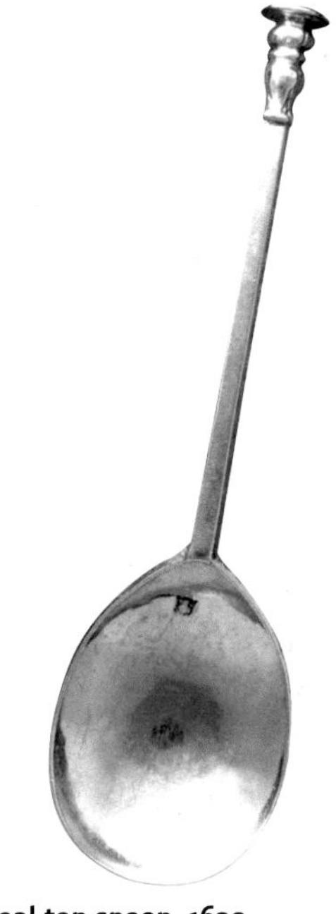
Seal top spoon, 1630

must know

From 1701 onwards, Exeter uses a 24-letter date sequence, omitting J and U.

From 1721 onwards, Exeter's standard marks are the three-towered castle, leopard's head and lion passant in square shields.

The leopard's head mark is dropped from 1778.

Exeter's wealth from this period comes from the wool trade and shipping.

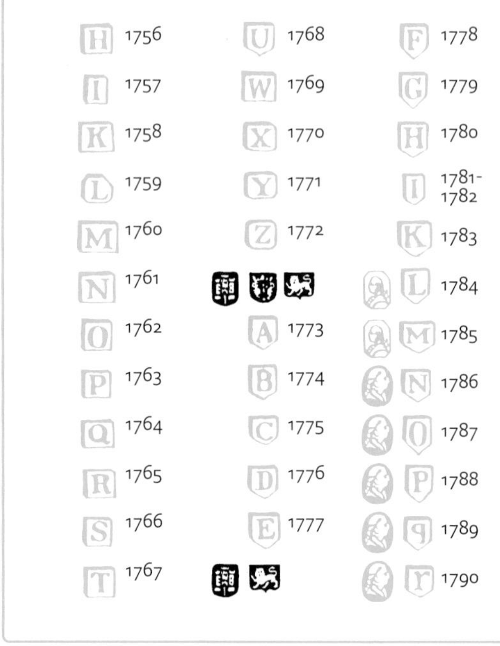

1791
1792
1793
1794
1795
1796
1797
1798
1799
1800
1801
1802
1803
1804
1805
1806
1807
1808
1809
1810
1811
1812
1813
1814
1815
1816
1817
1818
1819
1820
1821
1822
1823

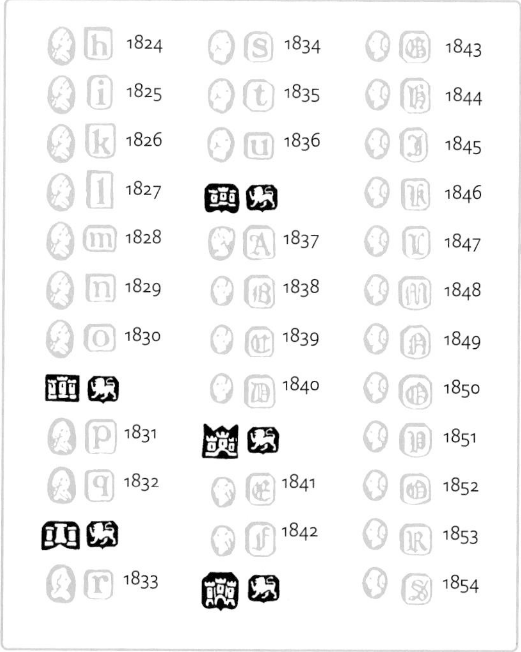

1824
1825
1826
1827
1828
1829
1830
1831
1832
1833
1834
1835
1836
1837
1838
1839
1840
1841
1842
1843
1844
1845
1846
1847
1848
1849
1850
1851
1852
1853
1854

must know

From 1797 onwards, Exeter uses a 20-letter date sequence from A to U, omitting J.

In 1837 the sovereign's head duty mark changes from William IV to Victoria, the first ruling queen of Britain for more than a century.

must know

Objects in the period 1485 to 1556 are known as Tudor style.

Date letter	Year
T	1855
U	1856
A	1857
B	1858
C	1859
D	1860
E	1861
F	1862
G	1863
H	1864
I	1865
K	1866
L	1867
M	1868
N	1869
O	1870
P	1871
Q	1872
R	1873
S	1874
T	1875
U	1876
A	1877
B	1878
C	1879
D	1880
E	1881
F	1882

Exeter Assay Office closed in 1883

Exeter makers' marks (A–W)

AR	Peter Arno
DC	Daniel Coleman
EI	John Elston
FR	Richard Freeman
GF	George Ferris
GT	George Turner
IB	John Buck
IE	John Elston
IP	Isaac Parkin
IW	John Williams
JH	Joseph Hicks
JO	John Osmont
JS	John Stone or James Strong
JW	James Williams
JW & Co	James Whipple & Co
Mo	John Mortimer
RF	Richard Ferris
Ri	Edward Richards
RS	Richard Sams
SB	Samuel Blachford
SL	Simon Lery
Sy	Pentycost Symonds
TB	Thomas Blake
TE	Thomas Eustace
TR	George Trowbridge
TS	Thomas Sampson
Wi	Richard Wilcocks
WP	William Parry or William Pearse or William Pope
WRS	W R Sobey
WW	William West

John Elston

John Mortimer

Pentycost Symonds

Thomas Eustace

Dublin

Dublin's Goldsmiths' Company was given its charter in 1638, although silver had been made there long before and the sterling standard was adopted as early as 1606. Dublin silver is known for a high standard of decorative workmanship.

The mark of origin is a crowned harp. Originally it also doubled as the standard mark. From 1731 the figure of Hibernia duty mark was added. From 1807 the sovereign's head mark became the duty mark (up to 1890, as in England), Hibernia was kept, and in time became regarded as the mark of origin, with the harp crowned as the sterling standard mark.

must know

Two different versions of the crowned harp mark of origin are used up until 1719.

Sterling silver oval basket, 1792

1670	1680	1703
	1681	1704–05
1671	1682	1706–07
1672	1683–84	1708–09
1673	1685–87	1710–11
1674	1688–93	1712–13
1675	1694–95	
1676	1696–98	1714
1677	1699	1715
	1700	1716
1678	1701	
1679	1702	1717

must know

From 1717–19, an aborted three-letter date sequence of A to C was used, interrupting the usual 23- or 24-letter date sequence omitting J, V and sometimes I; the letter L was repeated in 1730 and 1731 and two different shields were used in both 1740 and 1741–42.

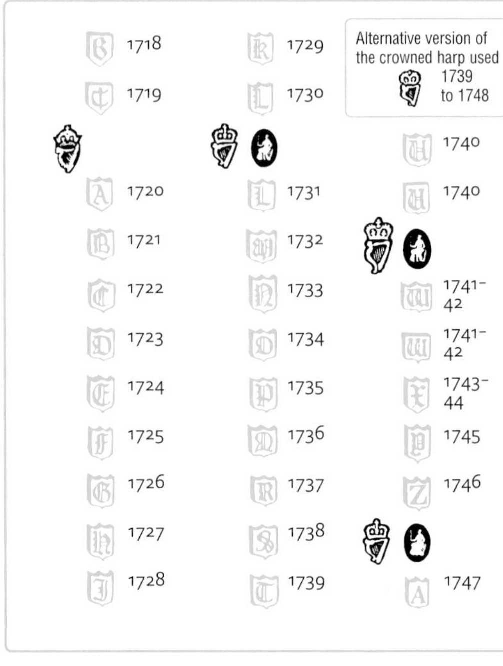

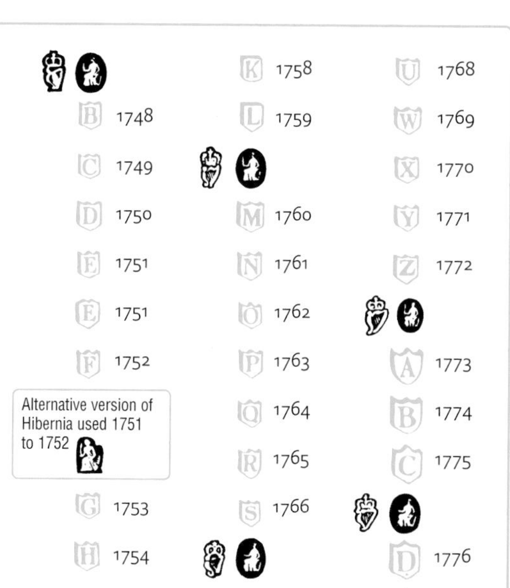

Hook end soup ladle, 1762

1778	1789	1799
1779	1790	1800
1780	1791	1801
1781	1792	1802
1782	1793	1803
1783	1794	1804
1784	1795	1805
1785	1796	1806
1786	1797	1807
1787	1798	1808
1788		1809

must know

The sovereign's head duty mark first appeared in 1807; Hibernia was retained but was considered as a mark of origin for Dublin.

must know

In 1821 a 25-letter date sequence omitting the letter J is adopted. Two versions of the letter E are used in 1825.

From 1851 to 1853, the letters F, G and G appear in two differently-shaped shields each year.

1810
1811
1812
1813
1814
1815
1816
1817
1818
1819
1820

1821
1822
1823
1824
1825
1825
1826
1827
1828

1829
1830
1831
1832
1833
1834
1835
1836

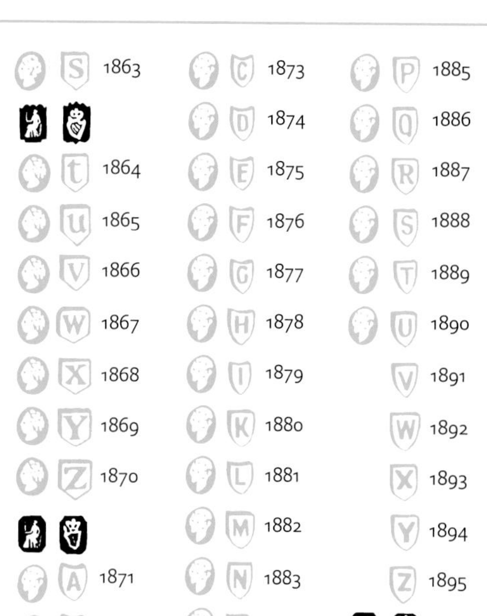

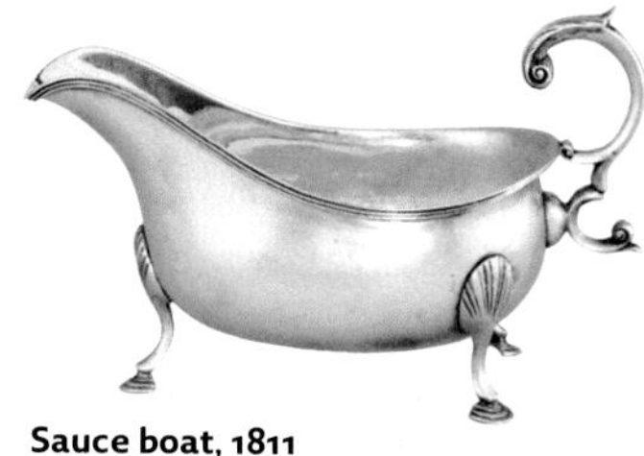

Sauce boat, 1811

1896	1908	1919
1897	1909	1920
1898	1910	1921
1899	1911	1922
1900	1912	1923
1901	1913	1924
1902	1914	1925
1903	1915	1926
1904		1927
1905	1916	1928
1906	1917	1929
1907	1918	1930-31

must know

In 1922 the 26 southern counties of Ireland become the Irish Free State, an independent dominion within the British Commonwealth. The country is renamed Eire in 1937 and in 1949 leaves the Commonwealth to become the Republic of Ireland.

must know

Commemorative marks are used in both 1966 and 1973.

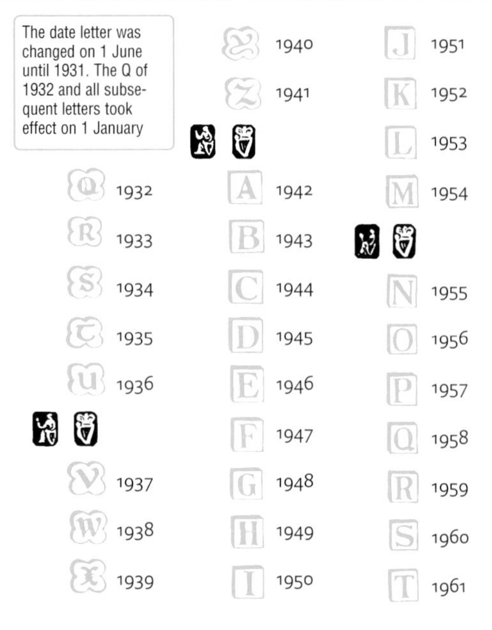
The date letter was changed on 1 June until 1931. The Q of 1932 and all subsequent letters took effect on 1 January
1932
1933
1934
1935
1936
1937
1938
1939
1940
1941
1942
1943
1944
1945
1946
1947
1948
1949
1950
1951
1952
1953
1954
1955
1956
1957
1958
1959
1960
1961

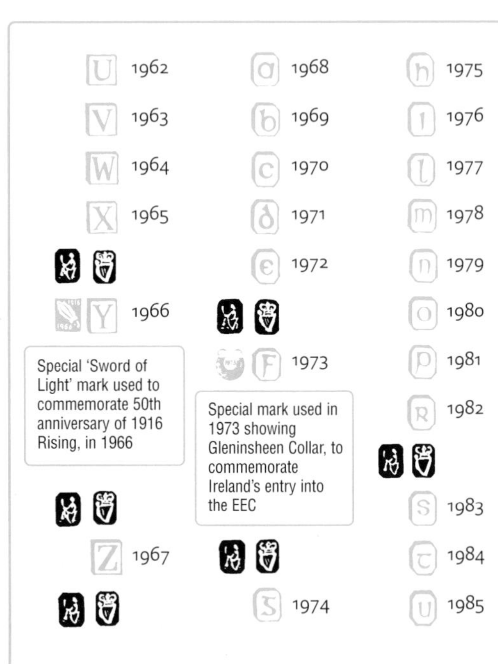
1962
1963
1964
1965
1966
Special 'Sword of Light' mark used to commemorate 50th anniversary of 1916 Rising, in 1966
1967
1968
1969
1970
1971
1972
1973
Special mark used in 1973 showing Gleninsheen Collar, to commemorate Ireland's entry into the EEC
1974
1975
1976
1977
1978
1979
1980
1981
1982
1983
1984
1985

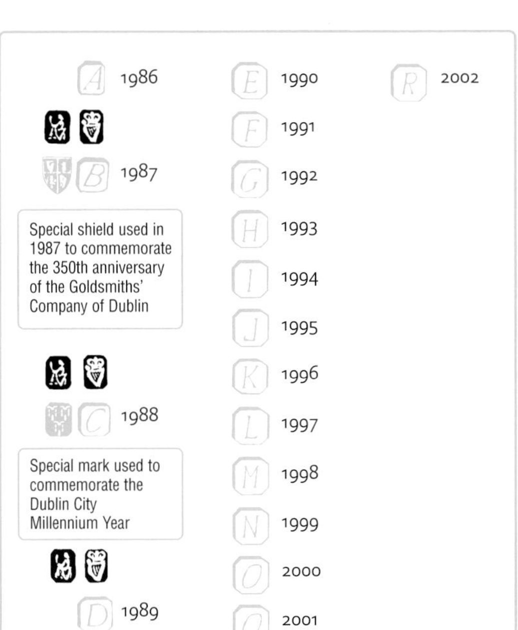

must know

Commemorative marks are used in 1987 and 1988.

Dublin makers' marks (A–W)

AB	Alexander Brown
AL	Antony Lefebure
AR	Alexander Richards
BM	Bartholomew Mosse
CM	Charles Marsh
CT	Christopher Thompson
DE	Daniel Egan
DK	David King
EB	Edward Barrett
EC	E Crofton
EF	Esther Forbes
EJ	Edmund Johnson
EP	Edward Pome
GA	George Alcock
GW	George Wheatley
HM	Henry Matthews
IB	John Buckton
IC	John Cuthbert or John Christie
IF	John Fry
IH	John Hamilton
II	Joseph Jackson
IL	John Laughlin
ILB	John Le Bas
IP	John Pittar
IS	James Scott
JD	James Douglas
JP	John Power
J.P	John Pittar
JS	James Smythe
MH	Michael Hewitson
MN	Michael Nowlan
MW	Matthew West
PM	Patrick Moore
PW	Peter Walsh
RC	Robert Calderwood
RS	Richard Sawyer
RW	Richard Williams or Robert William
SN	Samuel Neville
SW	Samuel Walker
TJ	Thomas Jones
TK	Thomas Kinslea
TP	Thomas Parker
TS	Thomas Slade
TW	Thomas Walker
TWY+	Edward Twycross
WA	William Archdall
WC	William Cummins
WL	William Lawson
WN	William Nowlan
WR	William Rose
WW	William Williamson

Newcastle

Silver was assayed in Newcastle from the mid-17th century, becoming systematic in 1702. Newcastle is known for domestic silver, tankards and two-handled cups. A curiosity of Newcastle is the presence of three known women silversmiths.

The town mark depicted three separate castles. From 1702 to 1719 the Britannia mark and the lion's head erased were in use until replaced in 1720 by the leopard's head and the lion passant. From 1721 to 1727 the lion passant usually faced to the right. The sovereign's head duty mark was used from 1784 to 1883.

must know

Dating Newcastle silver before the introduction of date marks in 1702 is difficult, as the three-castle town mark is often used for several years. Marks of this period will also be faint or worn.

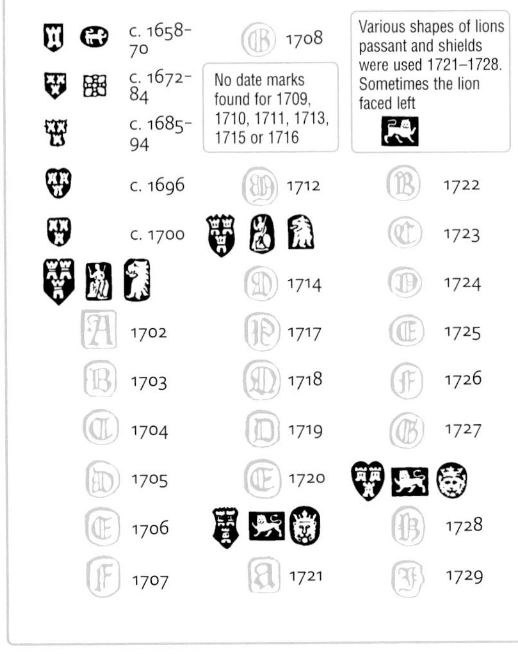

Straight-sided mug by Issac Cookson, 1753

1772
1773
1774
1775
1776
1777
1778
1779
1780
1781
1782
1783
1784
1785
1786
1787
1788
1789
1790
1791
1792
1793
1794
1795
1796
1797
1798
1799
1800
1801
1802
1803
1804

must know

The date letter sequence began in 1702. Newcastle used a 19-letter sequence (A to T generally omitting J) until 1759, when a 24-letter sequence was introduced (omitting J and V). The date letter was changed in May.

must know

Newcastle marks of this period are large and clear, so are easy to distinguish and date.

Letter	Year	Letter	Year	Letter	Year
P	1805	B	1816	O	1828
Q	1806	C	1817	P	1829
R	1807	D	1818	Q	1830
S	1808	E	1819	R	1831
T	1809	F	1820	S	1832
U	1810	G	1821	T	1833
W	1811	H	1822	U	1834
X	1812	I	1823	W	1835
Y	1813	K	1824	X	1836
Z	1814	L	1825	Y	1837
		M	1826	Z	1838
A	1815	N	1827		

Letter	Year	Letter	Year	Letter	Year
A	1839	L	1850	Y	1862
B	1840	M	1851	Z	1863
C	1841	N	1852		
D	1842	O	1853	a	1864
E	1843	P	1854	b	1865
F	1844	Q	1855	c	1866
G	1845	R	1856	d	1867
		S	1857	e	1868
H	1846	T	1858	f	1869
I	1847	U	1859	g	1870
J	1848	W	1860	h	1871
K	1849	X	1861	i	1872

Silver sugar spoon, c. 1856

must know

The last date mark for Newcastle gold and silver is 1883, as the assay office closes the following year.

Newcastle makers' marks (A–Y)

AK	Alexander Kelty
AR	Anne Robertson
Ba	Francis Batty
Bi	Eli Bilton
Bu	John Buckle
CJR	Christian Reid Junior
CR	Christian & David Reid
CR IS	Christian Reid & John Stoddart
DC	David Crawford
DD	David Darling
DL	Dorothy Langlands
DR	David Reid
FB	Francis Batty
GB	George Bulman
IC	Isaac Cookson
IK	James Kirkup
IL IR	John Langlands & John Robertson
IM	John Mitchison
IR	John Robertson
IS	John Stoddart
IW	John Walton
La	John Langwith
L & S	Lister & Sons
MA	Mary Ashworth
Ra	John Ramsay
R & D	Robertson & Darling
RM	Robert Makepeace
RP RS	Pinkney & Scott
RS	Robert Scott
TP	Thomas Partis
TS	Thomas Sewill
TW	Thomas Watson
WL	William Lister
WL CL WL	Lister & Sons
WR	William Ramsay
Yo	John Younghusband

Francis Batty

Lister & Sons

William Ramsay

Chester

Chester is known for small items such as beakers and creamers. From the early 15th century, Chester's guild of goldsmiths supervised the trade, until regulation in the late 17th century.

The mark of origin was the city arms, a sword between three wheatsheaves (gerbes), changed in 1701 to three wheatsheaves halved with three lions halved. From 1701 to 1718 the figure of Britannia and the lion's head erased were used as the standard mark and from 1719 the crowned leopard's head and the lion passant. From 1839 the leopard's head was omitted.

Standing paten, 1723-24

Mark	Year	Mark	Year	Mark	Year
	1680	I	1709	U	1720
	1690	K	1710	V	1721
STER LING	c. 1690–1700	L	1711	W	1722
		M	1712	X	1723
A	1701	N	1713	Y	1724
B	1702	O	1714	Z	1725
C	1703	P	1715		
D	1704	Q	1716	A	1726
E	1705	R	1717	B	1727
F	1706	S	1718	C	1728
G	1707			D	1729
H	1708	T	1719	E	1730

must know

Dating Chester silver is difficult before 1701, as the town's assay office did not use date marks.

Letter	Year	Letter	Year	Letter	Year
F	1731	S	1743	c	1753
G	1732	T	1744	d	1754
H	1733	U	1745	e	1755
I	1734	V	1746	f	1756
K	1735	W	1747	G	1757
L	1736	X	1748	h	1758
M	1737	Y	1749	i	1759
N	1738	Y	1749	k	1760
O	1739	Z	1750	l	1761
P	1740			m	1762
Q	1741	a	1751	n	1763
R	1742	b	1752	o	1764

must know

Two versions of the letter Y are used in 1749.

The letter T is repeated in 1769 and 1770.

The St Martin cup, 1755–56

Letter	Year	Letter	Year	Letter	Year
P	1765	a	1776	l	1786
Q	1766	b	1777	m	1787
R	1767	c	1778	n	1788
S	1768			o	1789
T	1769	d	1779	p	1790
T	1770	e	1780	q	1791
U	1771	f	1781	r	1792
V	1772	g	1782	s	1793
W	1773	h	1783	t	1794
X	1774			u	1795
Y	1775	i	1784	v	1796
		k	1785		

Parcel gilt mug, 1771–72

must know

A 21-letter date sequence omitting J and ending at V is used between 1797 and 1817.

The leopard's head standard mark is omitted from Chester hallmarks after 1839.

Chester does not change the sovereign's head duty mark until 1839, two years after the accession of Queen Victoria.

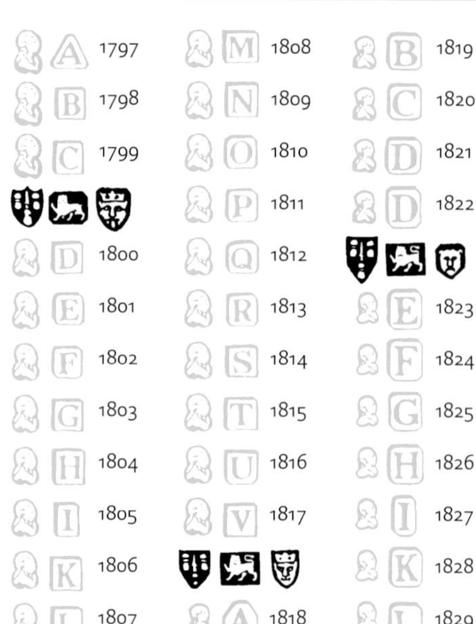

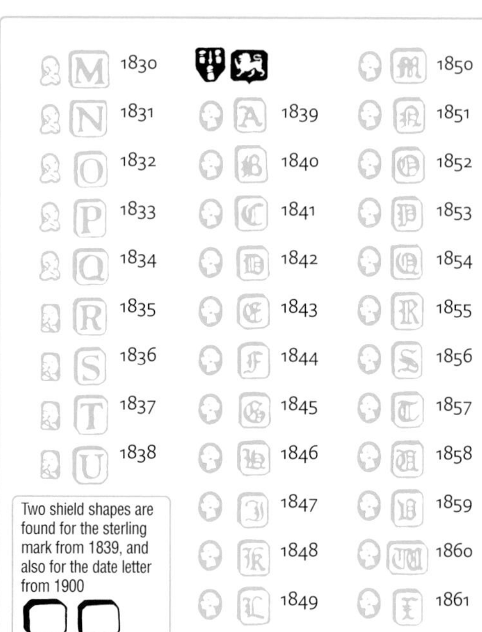

Two shield shapes are found for the sterling mark from 1839, and also for the date letter from 1900

Pair of bon-bon dishes, 1925

must know

A 25-letter dating sequence omitting J is in used at this period.

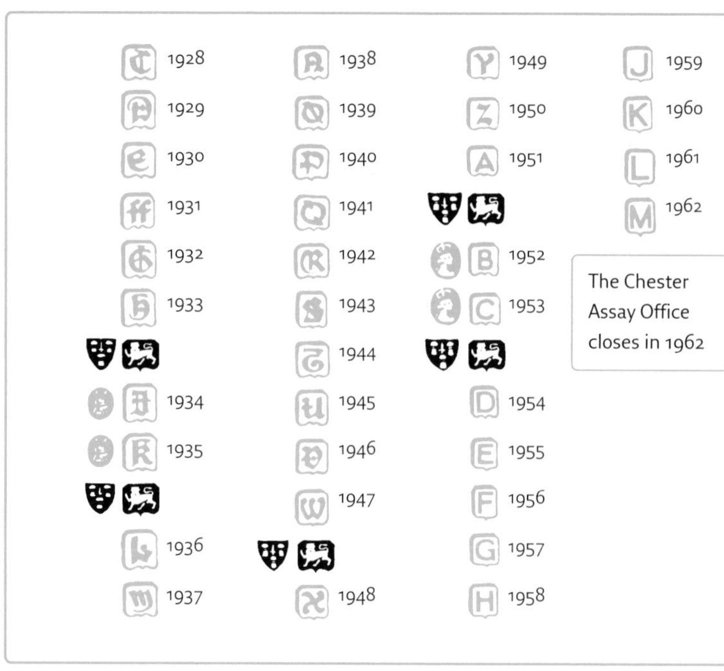

Chester makers' marks (A–W)

B & F	Matthew Boulton & James Fothergill
Bi	Charles Bird
BP	Benjamin Pemberton
Bu	Nathaniel Bullen
Du	Bartholomew Duke
EM	Edward Maddock
FB	Francis Butt
GL	George Lowe
GR	George Roberts
GW	George Walker
IB	James Barton
IG	John Gilbert
IL TL	John & Thomas Lowe
IR	John Richards
IW	Joseph Walley
JA	John Adamson
JC	James Conway or john Coakley
JL	John Lowe
JS	John Sutters
NC	Nicholas Cunliffe
Pe	Peter Pemberton
RG	Robert Green
RI	Robert Jones
RL	Robert Lowe
RP	Richard Pike
RR	Richard Richardson
TM	Thomas Maddock
WH	William Hull
WP	William Pugh
WR	William Richardson

Nicholas Cunliffe

Richard Richardson

Thomas Maddock

Glasgow

Silver was assayed in Glasgow from the late 17th century, although in the years 1784–1819 Glasgow silverware was mainly assayed in Edinburgh. In 1819 the Glasgow Goldsmiths' Company was formed and several changes were made in the marks.

The Glasgow mark of origin was a tree with a bird in the upper branches, a bell hanging from a lower branch and a fish (with a ring in its mouth) laid across the trunk. From 1819 a lion rampant was adopted as the sterling standard mark, and the Britannia standard and appropriate mark were in optional use. In 1914 the Scottish thistle was added.

George III plaid brooch, 1773

must know

The sovereign's head duty mark was used from 1819 to 1890.

Plaid brooch, 1832

must know

Between 1784 and 1819, most Glasgow silverware is assayed in Edinburgh.

Unusually, Glasgow uses the full 26-letter date sequence from 1819 onwards.

1883	1895	1906
1884	1896	1907
1885		1908
1886	1897	1909
1887	1898	1910
1888	1899	1911
1889	1900	1912
1890	1901	1913
1891	1902	
1892	1903	1914
1893	1904	1915
1894	1905	1916

must know

The Scottish thistle mark is added alongside the sterling standard mark from 1914.

Commemorative marks are added in both 1934 and 1935.

1917	1928	1938
1918	1929	1939
1919	1930	1940
1920	1931	1941
1921	1932	1942
1922	1933	1943
		1944
1923	1934	1945
1924	1935	1946
1925		1947
1926	1936	1948
1927	1937	

Caddy spoon, 1930

must know

The last Glasgow date mark is 1963, as the city's assay office closes in 1964.

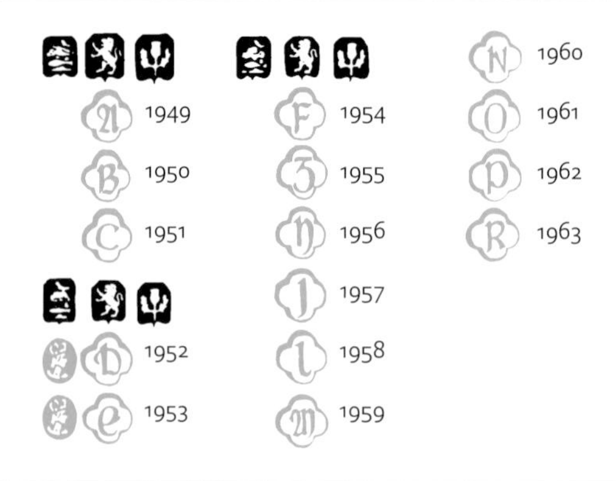

Glasgow makers' marks (A–W)

AM	Alexander Mitchell
A & T	Aird & Thompson
DCR	Duncan Rait
DMcD	David McDonald
JC	James Crichton
JL	John Law
JM	John Mitchell or J Murray
LFN	Luke Newlands
PA	Peter Arthur
RG & S	Robert Gray & Sons
WP	William Parkins

Alexander Mitchell

Ducan Rait

John Mitchell

Robert Gray & Sons

William Parkins

Birmingham

The Birmingham Assay Office opened in 1773, after which the city quickly grew in importance as a centre of silversmithing.

The mark of origin is an anchor (struck lying on its side for gold and platinum). It appeared very consistently with the lion passant standard mark. The sovereign's head duty mark was in use from 1784 to 1890.

A special commemorative mark was struck in 1973 to mark the bicentenary of the Birmingham Assay Office. Platinum was first assayed here in 1975 and the office is still in operation today.

must know

Along with Sheffield, Birmingham is the most recent of the assay offices, opening in 1773.

The 25-letter date sequence from 1773 to 1797 is followed by a 26-letter sequence.

must know

One of Birmingham's most famous silversmiths, Matthew Boulton, dies in 1809. In 1762 he had become the first person outside Sheffield to manufacture Sheffield plate and had campaigned for an assay office in Birmingham.

The date sequence in operation from 1824 to 1848 is often difficult to read because of its gothic type.

1802
1803
1804
1805
1806
1807
1808
1809
1810
1811
1812
1813
1814
1815
1816
1817
1818
1819
1820
1821
1822
1823
1824
1825
1826
1827
1828
1829
1830
1831
1832
1833
1834
1835
1836

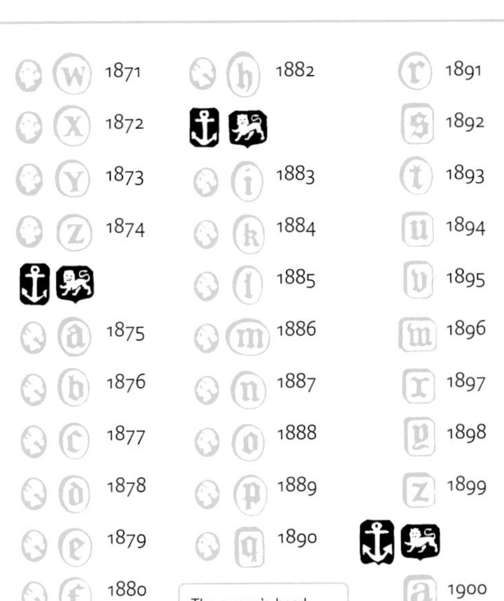

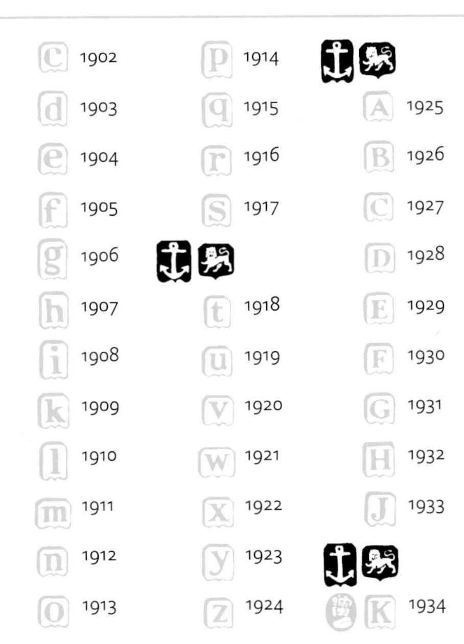

must know

The date letter sequence began in 1773 (in which year the letter A appeared in three different shapes of shield). Birmingham used 25 and 26-letter sequences alternately (omitting J).

25-letter date sequences omitting I or J are used after 1875 up to the present day.

Salt cellars, c. 1873

Prize medal, c. 1931

Whisky flask, 1940

1935	1946	1955
1936	1947	1956
1937	1948	1957
1938	1949	1958
1939	1950	1959
1940	1951	1960
1941	1952	1961
1942	1953	1962
1943	1954	1963
1944		1964
1945		1965

must know

The date letter was changed annually in July until 1975, since when all British date letters have been standardised, changing on 1 January.

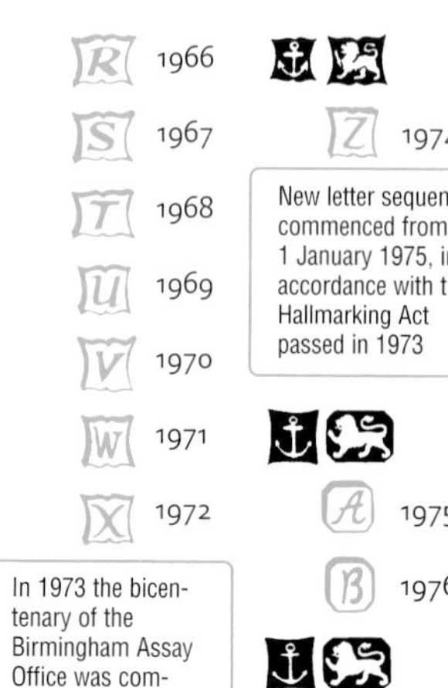

1966	1974	1979
1967	1975	1980
1968	1976	1981
1969	1977	1982
1970	1978	1983
1971		1984
1972		1985
1973		1986
		1987
		1988
		1989
		1990

New letter sequence commenced from 1 January 1975, in accordance with the Hallmarking Act passed in 1973

In 1973 the bicentenary of the Birmingham Assay Office was commemorated by a special town mark

Mark	Year
R	1991
S	1992
T	1993
U	1994
V	1995
W	1996
X	1997
Y	1998
Z	1999
a	2000
b	2001
c	2002

The Birmingham Assay Office is one of four British assay offices still in operation today.

Gilt ormulu plaque of Mathew Boulton

Birmingham makers' marks (C–Y)

C & B	Cocks & Bettridge
E & Co Ld	Elkington & Co. Ltd
EM & Co	Elkington Mason & Co.
ES	Edward Smith
ET	Edward Thomason
FC	Francis Clark
GU	George Unite
GW	Gervase Wheeler
H & T	Hilliard & Thomason
IB	John Bettridge
IS	John Shaw
IT	Joseph Taylor
JW	Joseph Willmore
L & Co	John Lawrence & Co.
MB	Matthew Boulton
MB IF	Matthew Boulton & John Fothergill
ML	Matthew Linwood
NM	Nathaniel Mills
P & T	William Postan & George Tye
REA	Robinson, Edkins Aston
SP	Samuel Pemberton
T & P	Joseph Taylor & John Perry
TS	Thomas Shaw
TW	Thomas Willmore
WF	William Fowke
Y & W	Yapp & Woodward

Gervase Wheeler

Mathew Boulton & John Fothergill

Thomas Willmore

Sheffield

Sheffield Assay Office was opened in 1773. The city is best known for the production of candlesticks.

The mark of origin on Sheffield silver was the crown, but this changed to a York rose in 1975. The standard mark was a lion passant. The sovereign's head duty mark was in use from 1784 to 1890.

From 1780 to 1853 small items were marked with a special stamp combining the crown mark of origin and the date letter.

The use of date letters began in September 1773 with the letter E, changing every July. The choice of letter was quite random until 1824.

must know

Date marks at this period are quite random, which makes dating difficult without a reference book.

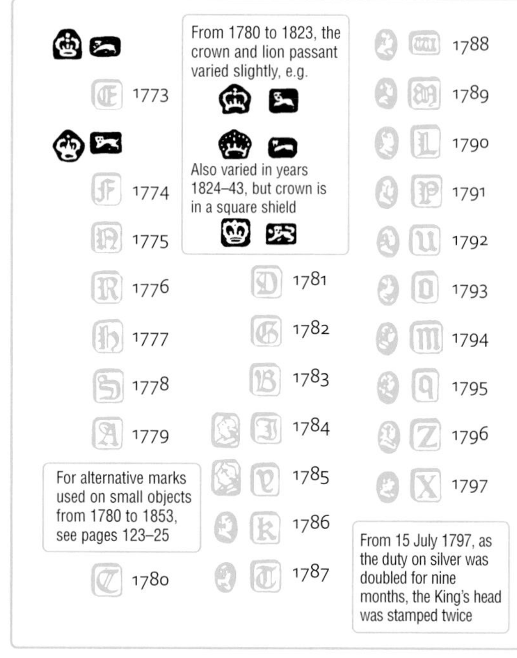

Letter	Year	Letter	Year	Letter	Year
V	1798	L	1810	Z	1822
E	1799	C	1811	U	1823
N	1800	D	1812	a	1824
H	1801	R	1813	b	1825
M	1802	W	1814	c	1826
F	1803	O	1815	d	1827
G	1804	T	1816	e	1828
B	1805	X	1817	f	1829
A	1806	I	1818	g	1830
S	1807	V	1819	h	1831
P	1808	Q	1820	k	1832
K	1809	Y	1821	l	1833

must know

In 1824 Sheffield began to use a regular 25-letter alphabetical sequence (omitting J), changing in July.

In 1975 the standard British date letter sequence was imposed, with the letter being changed on 1 January each year.

Small mugs, 1826

Letter	Year	Letter	Year	Letter	Year
m	1834	B	1845	O	1857
p	1835	C	1846	P	1858
q	1836	D	1847	R	1859
r	1837	E	1848	S	1860
s	1838	F	1849	T	1861
t	1839	G	1850	U	1862
u	1840	H	1851	V	1863
v	1841	I	1852	W	1864
x	1842	K	1853	X	1865
z	1843	L	1854	Y	1866
		M	1855	Z	1867
A	1844	N	1856		

must know

It is easy to identify a small piece of Georgian silver as coming from Sheffield, as date letters between 1780 and 1828 are shown with a crown above them.

From 1829 to 1853 small pieces of Sheffield silver are marked with the crown to the left or right of the date letter.

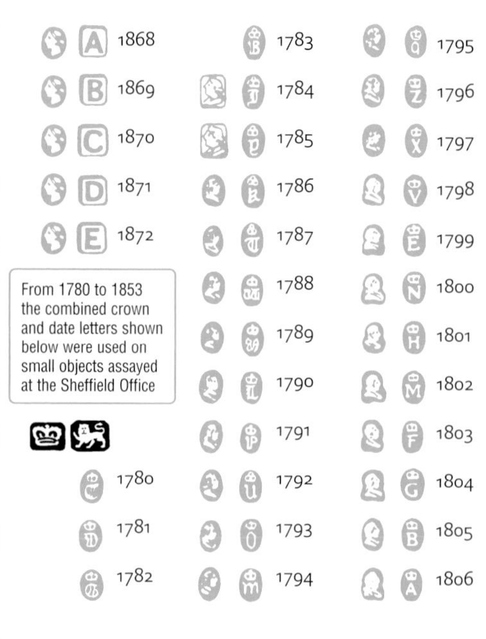

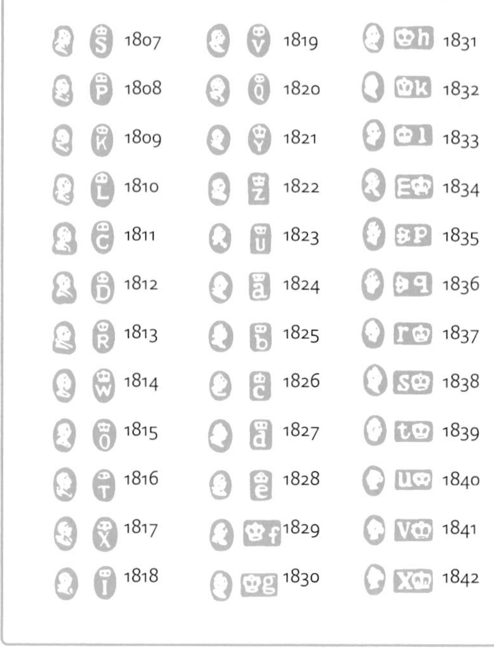

Letter	Year	Letter	Year	Letter	Year
Z	1843	F	1873	S	1885
A	1844	G	1874	T	1886
B	1845	H	1875	U	1887
C	1846	J	1876	V	1888
D	1847	K	1877	W	1889
E	1848	L	1878	X	1890
F	1849	M	1879	Y	1891
G	1850	N	1880	Z	1892
H	1851	O	1881	a	1893
I	1852	P	1882	b	1894
K	1853	Q	1883	c	1895
		R	1884		

Letter	Year	Letter	Year	Letter	Year
d	1896	q	1908	b	1919
e	1897	r	1909	c	1920
f	1898	s	1910	d	1921
g	1899	t	1911	e	1922
h	1900	u	1912	f	1923
i	1901	v	1913	g	1924
k	1902	w	1914	h	1925
l	1903	x	1915	i	1926
m	1904	y	1916	k	1927
n	1905	z	1917	l	1928
o	1906	a	1918	m	1929
p	1907			n	1930

must know

Between 1780 and 1853 many small Sheffield pieces have a combined date, letter and hallmark in one punch.

Shaving brush container, 1902

Edwardian silver cream jug, 1907

Art deco inkstand, 1931

O 1931	Y 1941	
P 1932	Z 1942	K 1952
q 1933		L 1953
	A 1943	
r 1934	B 1944	M 1954
s 1935	C 1945	N 1955
	D 1946	O 1956
t 1936	E 1947	P 1957
u 1937	F 1948	Q 1958
v 1938	G 1949	R 1959
w 1939	H 1950	S 1960
x 1940	I 1951	T 1961

must know

In 1975 Sheffield changes its mark of origin from a crown to a York rose.

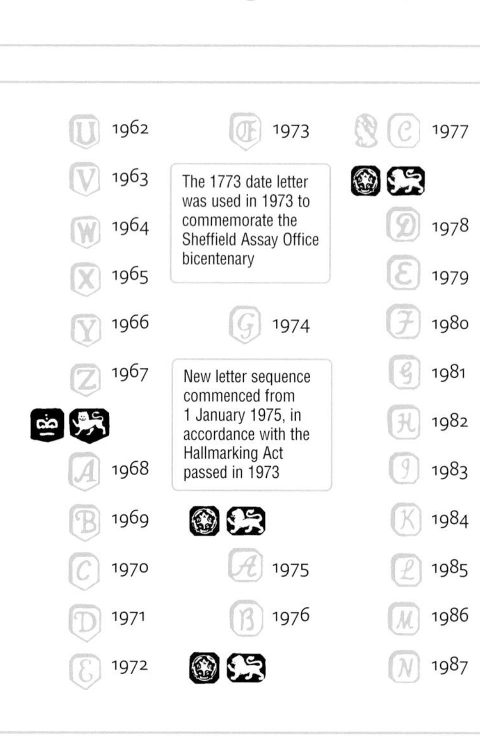

O	1988	S	1992	W	1996
P	1989	T	1993	X	1997
Q	1990	U	1994	Y	1998
R	1991	V	1995	Z	1999

must know

The Sheffield Assay Office is still in operation.

Sheffield makers' marks (A–W)

AH	Aaron Hadfield
DH & Co	Daniel Holy & Co.
D & S	Dixon & Sons
GA & Co	George Ashforth & Co.
GE & Co	George Eadon & Co.
HA	Henry Archer & Co.
H & H	Howard & Hawksworth
HE & Co	Hawksworth, Eyre & Co.
HT	Henry Tudor
HW & Co	Henry Wilkinson & Co.
IG & Co	John Green & Co.
IH & Co	J Hoyland & Co.
IL	John Law
IP & Co	John Parsons & Co.
IR & Co	John Roberts & Co.
ITY & Co	John T Younge & Co.
IW & Co	John Winter & Co.
JB	James Burbury
JC NC	J & N Creswick
JD & S	James Dixon & Sons
JR	J Round & Son
MF	Fenton, Creswick
RC	& Co.
MH & Co	Martin Hall & Co.
NS & Co	Nathaniel Smith & Co.
RM	Richard Morton
RM & Co	Richard Morton & Co.
RM EH	Remy Martin & Edward Hall
S & N	Stafford & Newton
SR & Co	Samuel Roberts & Co.
T & IS	T & I Settle
TJ NC	TJ & N Creswick
WD	William Damant
WF AF	Fordham & Faulkner
W & H	Walker & Hall

American gold and silver

The first evidence of gold and silver working in the Americas consists of thin, worked, gold foil in the hands of a man buried along with his tool kit in the highlands of Peru before 1500 BCE.

Gold breast ornament from coastal Ecuador, 500–1500 CE

More substantial evidence comes from the extravagant work of the Chimu people of Peru, from about 800 BCE. The craft spread slowly southwards to northern Argentina and northwards to Colombia towards the end of the last millennium BCE, and then into Central America in the early centuries CE.

Working precious metals

Gold deposits were found in the alluvium-rich rivers of the highlands and in veins of quartz in the hills. Silver and copper were also mined. Small furnaces were used to smelt the gold, which was then hammered into sheets over an anvil. While the use of sheet gold continued in the Andes and southern Colombia, casting was developed in northern Colombia and Central America, and some objects combined both techniques. Skills became more sophisticated, with objects made by various methods, using different metals and precious stones. Many spectacular 'gold' pieces were in fact made of thin sheets of gold plated over an alloy base.

Although a few practical objects were produced, most gold was used to make objects symbolizing supernatural power and its associated earthly, lordly status. Mythological beings and motifs were often shown, as intermediaries between gods and humans. Gold was most usually associated with the Sun, life and the production of food. It needed to

must know

The most advanced metal workers in the Americas were the Incas. They developed the production and use of alloys, notably bronze, and perfected the technique of inlaying one or more different metals.

Casting is the process of filling a cavity in a mould with molten metal to produce a finished piece (see page 120).

imitate divine light: to Incas, gold was 'the sweat of the Sun' and silver 'the tears of the moon'.

Spanish domination

For the peoples of the Americas, gold and silver had no worth in itself but was valued for what they depicted and for how they were thought to work. Items were often traded over hundreds of miles.

In the early 16th century, Spanish conquistadors swept away the Aztec and Inca empires and imposed Spanish rule. The Spanish valued gold for its own sake, and ransacked ancient tombs and burial sites looking for it. Centuries' worth of skills disappeared as the gold and later silver made Spain the richest nation in the world.

The Spanish were driven by the search for El Dorado, a fabled city of gold, itself inspired by a ceremony that took place on Lake Guatavita, north of Bogotá in Colombia, on the succession of a new Muisca (or Chibcha) ruler.

North America

Only in North America was there no native metal working tradition, until the arrival of silver from Mexico after 1853, when tribes in the south-western states of the USA, notably the Navajo and Pueblo, began to make jewellery. US and Mexican coins were a good source of silver. The finished items bore little relation to native styles and were increasingly produced using non-Amerindian craftworkers. Some of the tribes, including the Zuni, used silver as a base for polished stones, particularly turquoise, and shells, while the Hopi, taught by the Zuni, evolved a distinctive overlay technique by piercing a pattern through a sheet of silver and then soldering it to a flat base.

must know

The Spanish opened up new gold and silver mines, notably in 1545 at Potosi in southern Bolivia, the biggest single source of silver ever known. From Central America alone, 2812 tonnes of silver and 24 tonnes of gold were extracted during the 17th century, rising to 32,488 tonnes of silver and 91 tonnes of gold during the 19th century. Most was shipped back to Spain; with a little worked locally in Spanish styles.

While the Navajo were in exile from their homeland between 1864 and 1868, textiles - in particular blankets - ceased to have any spiritual significance to them. Instead, they began to make silver jewellery.

The Pueblo were village-based and were influenced by, and sometimes converted to, Roman Catholicism. They therefore often used the cross as an ornament.

African gold

The main gold fields in Africa are along the upper reaches of the Senegal, Niger and Volta rivers in West Africa, east of lakes Tanganyika and Malawi in East Africa, and between the Zambezi and Limpopo rivers, and in the Witwatersrand area of Transvaal in southern Africa. In all but the last case, the mining and trading of gold led to the development of major African civilizations.

must know

Gold jewellery from Mali is forged rather than cast and is often Arabian in style with much filigree work.

The Swahili people, of mixed Black African, Arab and Persian descent, dominated the ports of East Africa.

The first gold fields to be developed were in West Africa. Here the gold was taken north to market towns such as Timbuktu and Jenne along the Niger river in the Sahel (the grassland southern edge of the Sahara Desert), and from there by camel to North Africa for shipment, mainly to Europe. Until American gold became available in the 16th century, Europe relied almost entirely on West Africa for its gold supply. Ghana was the first kingdom to grow rich on its gold trade, in the 8th century. From the 13th century, the region was dominated by the Mali empire and later the Songhai empire (also in modern Mali).

In southern and eastern Africa, gold, ivory and other goods were traded down the main rivers to the East African coast and the Swahili-dominated ports. Arab merchants traded the gold to India and on to China in return for spices, cloth, beads and manufactured goods. The major inland kingdom in this period was Great Zimbabwe, which flourished from the 12th century, its people mining gold from the hills.

The coming of the Portuguese and then other Europeans from the end of the 15th century disrupted these trading networks and eventually swept away the native African kingdoms both here and in West Africa and replaced them with European colonial rule by the end of the 19th century.

The main workers of gold were the Asante people of Ghana in West Africa, whose kingdom emerged at the start of the 18th century. They used the lost-wax process to cast their gold, a method developed by the people of Igbo-Ukwu in Nigeria during the 10th century for the casting of bronze and perfected by the people of Benin during the 16th century.

The process involves making a wax model of the item to be cast. The model is then covered with a clay mould in which a small hole is pierced. When the mould is heated, the wax inside melts and is poured out through this hole. Molten gold is then poured into the mould and, when it has cooled and hardened, the mould is broken and the object removed for polishing and, any further decorative work. An alternative, and possibly older method of casting is the lost-beetle process, which uses the same techniques as for lost-wax casting except that a real object, such as a beetle, flower, nut or seed is encased in the clay mould. When the mould is heated, the object inside turns to ash that is then tipped out, allowing the molten gold to flow into the mould and take the form of the former object.

The Asante used this process to make jewellery and state ceremonial regalia. They also perfected the technique of making engraved and decorated gold sheets that could be applied to cloth headdresses, wooden sword hilts, and other items. All these gold and gold-plated objects were worked with elaborate designs of symbolic significance, conveying the importance, dignity and authority of the Asantahene and his kingdom.

Gold ornament from West Africa

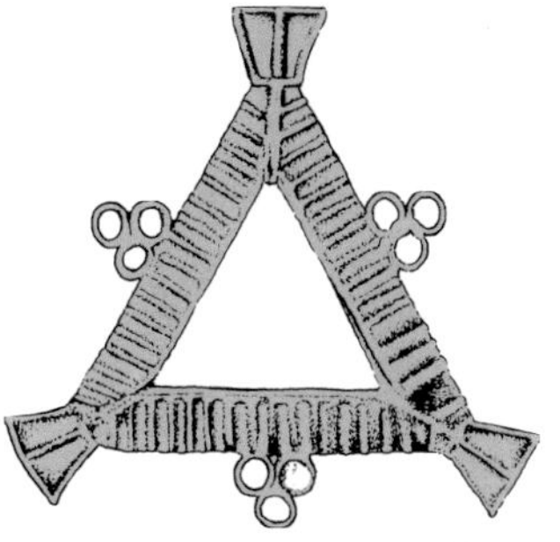

Weights used to measure gold dust or nuggets have been made and used by the Asante for centuries. The weights were produced by the lost wax or lost beetle process and are generally accurate to 0.2 oz (5.6 g).

Indian colonial gold and silver

The first Europeans to settle in India were the Portuguese, who established trading stations on the coast, notably at Goa, during the 16th century. British and French merchants followed them, the British setting up the East India Company in 1600 notably in Bombay, Calcutta and Madras.

must know

Most European silver imported into India kept its original European hallmarks, as there was a considerable cachet to anything made in Europe: to imply local manufacture would have downgraded the piece in the customer's eyes. Confusingly, however, imported plated silverware, such as candlesticks and candelabra but also larger pieces such as wine coolers, were often re-marked by the local retailer, making it difficult now to ascertain whether plated pieces are of colonial or European manufacture.

The first goldsmiths moved to India in the late 17th century. They had served their apprenticeship in England and were recruited by the East India Company at a fixed annual salary of around £50 to work as assayers or mint-masters. The first evidence of British goldsmiths working at their trade does not emerge in Madras until 1720. While we know their names from contemporary records and letters, we do not know what they produced, for there are no Indian assay marks.

This situation changed in the second half of the 18th century, when the British hold over India strengthened. The three main British settlements changed from being primarily military forts and trading stations to substantial residential cities. Goldsmiths now had a ready market for their wares and started to produce the first Indian silver of the colonial era. The climate and social habits of India required different items from those made in England: sauce or stew pans with removable or interchangeable handles for bringing curry to the table, long-handled toasting forks for cooking meat in front of a camp fire, silver-covered glass beakers for keeping out insects, and rice bowls. One of the most popular items was a set of muffineers or castors for salt, pepper and cayenne. These often travelled with their owner in his cummerbund. This required them to be cylindrical, their shape only changing in the 1840s.

Because most of the items made received considerable wear and tear both in the kitchen and through daily use, Indian silver tended to be thicker than its European counterpart. It was also regarded as second-rate, for European-produced silver and plated items had a prestige that local produce could never achieve. Silver was also imported from China, particularly to Bombay, where its low cost and superior quality restricted the development of colonial silver production.

Most Indian colonial silversmiths were English, although Scots formed a large contingent. There were also many Armenians, and a few Chinese.

While it is easy to identify Indian silver by its hybrid style, there is no single system of marks to help us date a piece, assay its purity or identify its origin. Most pieces bear a maker's mark of his initials, sometimes with an added symbol. Silversmiths from Aberdeen, notably John Mair in Calcutta and the Gordons in Madras, used a thistle.

Pieces from Calcutta dating from the early 19th century also carried a tally mark, enabling a workman to be identified and thus paid. Calcutta silver was also marked with the letters A or B. Although there were two standards of silver in use, the standard of silver used does not vary according to the mark. Silversmiths in Madras used only a maker's mark. Madras marks struck between 1830 and 1865 can easily be identified, as almost all have a line and two dots under the abbreviating 'o' of 'Co'.

must know

At the end of the 17th century, there was great demand for Chinese-style silver and gold in Europe. It is still unclear how much of this silver and gold was made by Europeans in India or imported direct from China itself.

European gold and silversmiths are also recorded in Agra, Allahabad, Bangalore, Benares, Cawnpore, Chittagong, Delhi, Lucknow, Mysore, Patna, Pondicherry, Rangoon, and Simla, as well as Penang and Singapore in Malaya, among other places.

Contemporary amulet box, India

Leading goldsmiths and silversmiths

James Aldridge (fl. 1778–1816) London silversmith whose work included articles decorated with engravings imitating contemporary Chinese designs, and porcelain pieces with silver mounts. William Beckford collected his work for Fonthill Abbey.

Angell Family of three generations of London silversmiths, descended from Joseph Angell, a weaver (d. c. 1830). Joseph Angell III (1816–1891) exhibited at the 1851 Great Exhibition and promoted the use of enamelling to decorate silverware, with mixed critical results.

Peter Archambo Two London silversmiths, father (fl. 1721–50) and son (1724–68) of Huguenot ancestry, renowned for their dinner plate.

Charles Robert Ashbee (1863–1942) Leading Art Nouveau silversmith and jewellery designer, originally an architect and goldsmith. In 1888 he founded the Guild and School of Handicraft in London, the school closing in 1895; in 1898 he registered the mark of the Guild of Handicraft, moving it to Chipping Camden, Glos, from 1902–08. He mainly designed tea services and other tableware, making much use of wirework.

Edward Barnard & Sons London firm of silversmiths, the successor to the firm started in 1689 by Anthony Nelme; taken over by Edward Barnard (1781–1846) and his three sons in 1829.

Bateman Family of London silversmiths, headed by Hester (née Needham, c. 1709–94) and her three sons John (d. 1778), Peter (1740–1825) and Jonathan (1747–91); between 1770–1810, the family firm were the most dominant silversmiths in England, producing some 11,000 pieces bearing the HB mark, mainly flatware, small jugs and salt cellars.

Vincenzo Belli (1710–87) Founder of a family of goldsmiths and silversmiths who made much of the best Roman domestic and ecclesiastical plate from the mid-18th to mid-19th centuries; his son Giovacchino (b. 1750) developed an antique revival style making sugar bowls in the shape of Grecian urns, etc.

Thomas Boulsover (1704–88) Sheffield cutler, in 1742 he discovered the process of making Sheffield Plate, which he called 'copper rolled plate'.

Matthew Boulton (1728–1809) Birmingham silversmith, industrialist and entrepreneur, becoming in 1762 the first person outside Sheffield to manufacture Sheffield plate: he developed the use of sterling silver around its edges to protect the plate at its hardest point of wear. As a silversmith he took design advice from Robert Adam and campaigned for local assay offices, as a result of which two were opened in Birmingham and Sheffield.

John Burt (c. 1692–1745) Apprentice of John Coney, he worked in Boston, Mass., and made silver for Harvard University; his three sons were also silversmiths, the youngest, Benjamin (1729–1805) leading the Boston goldsmiths at George Washington's memorial procession in 1800.

Benvenuto Cellini (1500–71) Florence-born goldsmith and sculptor, considered by many to be the finest and most famous goldsmith in the world. He trained and worked in Rome from 1519 as a goldsmith and medallist, moving to France to work for François I in 1540. Back in Rome in 1545, he wrote his autobiography and produced a number of fine gold pieces, although only one, an ornate salt cellar decorated with nude figures, a seahorse and dolphins, survives.

Chawner Family of London silversmiths: Thomas Chawner (1734–1805/11), his brother William (fl. 1759–84), born in Derbyshire, and his son Henry (1764–1851); William worked with George Heming to produce a dinner and dessert service for Catherine the Great of Russia.

John Coney (1655–1722) Boston, Mass. Born the son of emigrants from Lincolnshire, England and one of the most prolific New England silversmiths; he produced a wide range of domestic tableware, notably tankards and other drinking vessels, and in 1702 engraved the plates for the printing of paper money in Massachusetts.

Paul Crespin (1694–1770) London silversmith of Huguenot family, making many high-quality and finely executed pieces for the Portuguese royal family, members of the English nobility, and Catherine I of Russia.

James Dixon & Sons Leading 19th-century firm of Sheffield silversmiths, founded in 1806 by James Dixon (1776–1852).

Jeremiah Dummer (1645–1718) First native-born New England silversmith; among his surviving works are standing salts, a tankard with the cut-card decoration he is credited with introducing to America, and candlesticks.

John Flaxman (1755–1826) Noted sculptor and designer of silverware and ceramics in the neoclassical style, he worked closely with Josiah Wedgwood, for whom he designed a tea service.

William Garrett Forbes (1751–1840) Of Scottish and Dutch ancestry, William Forbes, his three sons, and a grandson were active in New York, initially producing silverware in the heavy Dutch style but later in a neoclassical style.

Garrard & Co Leading London gold and silversmiths, founded by George Wickes and Edward Wakelin in 1747; Robert Garrard (1758–1818) entered the business in 1792 and became sole owner in 1802. In 1818 he was succeeded by Robert Garrard II (1793–1881), the most famous silversmith in the family, renowned for his silver table centrepieces and figural pieces.

Gorham Leading American silverware firm of Providence, Rhode Island, founded in 1831 by Jabez Gorham (1792–1869) and famous for its spoons and hollow ware.

Pierre (or Peter) Harache London silversmiths, father (fl. 1682–98) and son

(1653–1717), of Huguenot descent, whose high-quality pieces are decorated with chasing, embossing, cut-card work, gadrooning, pierced work and cast mounts, although it is almost impossible to determine who was responsible for what, such is the similarity of design and mark.

F Antoine Heller (c. 1845–95) French silversmith who studied in Paris and went to the USA in the 1870s to work for Tiffany & Co. and then the Gorham Company, where he introduced a wide range of new flatware designs.

Thomas Heming (fl. 1745–73) London silversmith, appointed Principal Goldsmith to George III in 1760, for whom he made many important pieces, including regalia and plate for his coronation, as well as a dinner service for the Speaker of the House of Commons. His early work was in rococo style, although he became more restrained later. His son George (fl. 1773–93) continued his business, producing two complete dinner services for Catherine the Great.

Hennell Family firm of five generations of London silversmiths, founded by David Hennell (1712–85) and continuing until the death of his great-grandson in 1899.

John Hull (1624–83) Born Market Harborough, England, emigrated to America in 1635. In 1652 he minted the 'Pine Tree' shillings and sixpences in Massachusetts; Robert Sanderson was his partner, Jeremiah Dummer one of his apprentices.

Hunt & Roskell One of the most important 19th-century London silversmiths, founded by Paul Storr and John Mortimer in 1822; renamed by new partners in 1844 until bought by JW Benson in 1897.

Jacob Hurd (c. 1702–58) Boston, Mass. silversmith who made tableware, snuff boxes and sword hilts; over 300 pieces survive, including a gold snuff box in the Boston Museum of Fine Arts.

Thomas Jenkins (fl. 1668–1706) London silversmith, whose TI initials between scallop shells appear on more than 100 items of secular and church ware, including pieces with chinoiserie decoration.

Charles Kandler (fl. 1727–50) London silversmith who arrived from Germany in 1726, possibly related to Johann Kandler, the famous Meissen porcelain modeller; his few pieces are highly decorated in rococo style, some of which can be seen in the Hermitage Museum, St Petersburg.

Kirk Stieff Co Leading firm of silversmiths in Baltimore, Maryland and the oldest continuous firm in the USA, founded by Samuel Kirk (1793–1872) in 1815. Early work featured repoussé decoration, which it introduced to the USA before 1822, although other work is in neoclassical style, with chinoiserie motifs.

Paul de Lamerie (1688–1751) The most famous of all English goldsmiths, born in Holland and brought by his Huguenot parents to London in 1689. He registered his first maker's mark in 1713; was appointed Goldsmith to the King in 1716, and made many fine pieces for the Russian imperial court. His early work was in a restrained Queen Anne style, but by the 1730s he produced many large pieces, such as wine coolers and two-handed cups, in an exuberant rococo style.

Mappin & Webb Leading London firm of silversmiths, founded in Sheffield in 1774 by Jonathan Mappin and later joining with George Webb to open their first shop in London in 1862.

Myers Myer (1723-95) Leading New York silversmith of Sephardic Dutch origin, renowned for his synagogue pieces.

Anthony Nelme (fl. 1681–1722) Leading London silversmith, whose great quantity and variety of work was in the Restoration and Queen Anne styles; his son Francis (fl. 1719–39) succeeded him, largely using his father's models.

Abraham Lopes de Oliveyra (1657–1750) Probably the first Jewish silversmith to work in London after Jews were readmitted to the country in 1656, he was born in Amsterdam and came to London in 1697; he specialized in Jewish ritual silverware, although he also made secular ware.

Giovanni Battista Piranesi (1720–78) Italian designer and architect, whose silverware designs were based on antique images and which were worked up by leading European silversmiths of the day.

Augustus Pugin (1812–52) English architect and designer most famous for his decorative work on the rebuilt Houses of Parliament; he designed numerous pieces of silverware in Gothic style.

Omar Ramsden (1873–1939) Leading English silverware designer, born and apprenticed in Sheffield but working mostly in London with Alwyn Carr (1872–1940), his partner until 1919; his many ecclesiastical and secular designs were initially in the Arts and Crafts style, later showing Celtic influences.

Paul Revere (1735–1818) One of the most famous silversmiths in history, if only for his night-time ride on 18/19 April 1775 out of Boston to warn the American colonists that the British were coming, one of the most celebrated events in the American Revolution. Revere learned his trade from his father and became a fine engraver, later developing copper plate engraving for printing; his most famous piece is the 1786 gold Sons of Liberty Bowl.

Richardson Three generations of American Quaker gold- and silversmiths working in Philadelphia during the 18th century, noted for their domestic ware.

Rundell, Bridge & Rundell Most prestigious firm of London silversmiths in the first half of the 19th century, dating from c. 1745, and from 1785 a partnership between Philip Rundell (1743–1827) and John Bridge (1755–1834), becoming Rundell, Bridge & Rundell after Philip's nephew Edmund joined the partnership in 1805. The firm received many royal commissions and was Crown Jeweller for many years until its dissolution in 1842.

Robert Sanderson (1608–93) British-born silversmith who emigrated to New England after 1635, making him the earliest-known American goldsmith whose – mainly ecclesiastical – work survives.

Paul Storr (1771–1844) One of the outstanding and prolific English silversmiths of the early 19th century, Storr worked for and was associated with the royal goldsmiths Rundell, Bridge & Rundell from 1796–1819;

his work is distinguished by an elaborate neoclassical and rococo sculptural style.

Philip Syng (1703–89) Irish-born Philadelphia goldsmith, who made the inkstand used at the signing of the Declaration of Independence in 1776 and is known for his handsome salvers and tankards.

Tiffany & Co. Leading American silversmith and jewellery firm, founded by Charles Lewis Tiffany (1812–1902) in New York in 1837, famous for its Art Nouveau glass and silverware.

Christian van Vianen (1598–c. 1666) Dutch silversmith from Utrecht who around 1630 emigrated to England, where he received a number of commissions from Charles I, including a 17-piece silver altar service for St George's Chapel, Windsor for the Order of the Garter. He left England in 1643, just after the start of the civil war, and did not return again until the Restoration in 1660, working for Charles II as Silversmith in Ordinary to the King.

Antoine Vechte (1799–1868) French designer who moved to London in 1848 to work for Hunt & Roskell, developing an easier process of embossing than hammering from the back, by making a model and from it a base-metal mould and then beating the silver plate into the mould to create a positive pattern.

David Willaume (1658–1740) French Huguenot silversmith from Metz who emigrated to London sometime before 1686; the most prolific of Huguenot silversmiths, he pioneered the use of gadrooning and other new styles.

Edward Winslow (1669–1753) Boston, Mass. silversmith, probably an apprentice of Jeremiah Dummer, who made much of Massachusetts's early ecclesiastical plate and secular tableware.

Engraving showing various skills used in a goldsmith's shop, 1741

Goldsmiths' and silversmiths' terminology

acid-etched Copperplate engraving technique adapted by silversmiths in which acid eats into unprotected parts of the metal to form shallow patterns; recognisable by its blurred lines.
alloy Mixture of two or more compatible metals – or a metal and non-metal such as carbon – fused together to form a harder, more durable metal.
annealing Method by which silver and other metals under the hammer are kept malleable by heating them to about 700°C and then plunging them into cold water.
assay Analysis of silver, gold and platinum to check they have no more than the legally permitted proportion of alloy; confirmed by an assay office's mark.
base metal Common metals such as copper, lead, tin and zinc, as opposed to precious metals, such as silver, gold and platinum.
beading Edging of small, raised bead-like domes.
blade tail Metal shank of a knife blade running down the centre of a handle, secured by resin or pitch.
bloomed gold Textured finish on gold achieved by immersing it in acid to give a matt, pitted effect.
bright cut Method of engraving silver and gold that burnishes one side of the cut while picking out the other with a bevelled edge to give extra brilliance.
Britannia standard High silver content (95.84%) required by English law from 1697–1720, still in occasional use.
British Plate 1830s version of Sheffield Plate, using nickel silver – a silver-white alloy of copper, nickel and zinc – instead of pure copper as the core.
carat Measure of the proportion of gold in an alloy, expressed as the number of parts of gold in 24 parts of the alloy, e.g. an 18c piece contains 18 parts (75%) pure gold, 6 parts (25%) other metals. Also a measure of the weight of precious stones, especially diamonds.
cartouche Scrolled decoration as part of an ornamental panel or armorial engraving.
cast chasing Type of chasing used to sharpen or add decorative details to a piece made by casting.
casting Process of making and shaping a gold or silver object by pouring the molten metal into a hollow mould made from a model of the desired object, suspending a close-fitting object inside the mould and flowing the molten metal around it to produce a hollow, or 'open', final product.
chased Metal decorated with punches, hammers and other tools for fine raised designs.
chenier Decorative wire tubing.
close plating Sheet of cast metal, often steel, plated with thin sheets of silver by means of solder; mostly used for domestic

tableware that is likely to rust.

coin silver Piece containing 90% silver and 10% other metal. At one time the standard content of silver coins in England.

cut-card work Applied decoration of French Huguenot origin, c. 1660–1730, consisting of flat sections of very thin silver cut to a simple pattern and then soldered onto the object to be decorated.

cutlery Knives and other implements with a cutting edge, used for cutting, carving, serving and eating food. Forks and spoons are flatware, although the terms cutlery and flatware are often used interchangeably.

damascene Inlay of gold and silver beaten into an undercut groove in another metal.

date hallmark Letter of the alphabet stamped by an assay office on an article of gold or silver to indicate the year of assaying, which is not necessarily the same as the year in which the piece was made.

die-stamping Method of mechanically embossing metal with an engraved stamp.

double-plated Type of plated metal covered with a layer of silver on both sides, used for making hollow ware when both sides are on view.

electrolysis Process of gold or silver gilding by means of an electrical current passed through a molten or liquid solution that breaks it up into its constituent elements; an item placed in the solution is then gilded with either the positive- or negative-charged element.

electroplate Nickel or copper thinly coated with a layer of silver by electrochemical action, indicated by the stamped initials EP or EPNS (electroplated nickel silver). Items that have been gold-plated are marked with HGE (hard gold electroplated).

electrotyping Production process for making accurate copies of an original piece.

embossed Decoration beaten out from the back of the metal with punches or, since the end of the 19th century, semi-mechanically.

engraving Line decoration cut into the surface from the front.

etching Technique of decorating the surface of a metal by the use of acids.

filigree Type of decoration on metalware usually made by the use of fine plain, twisted, or plaited wire formed into a delicate and intricate design of foliate or geometric form. Filigree is used either as an openwork border or soldered to a flat metal surface.

filled See **loaded**

finial Knob as a terminal decoration in the form of a flower, fruit, nut, human figure, shell, etc., for lids of tea and coffee pots, stems of spoons, etc. Sometimes termed a 'knop'.

flat chasing Chasing in very low relief worked from the front and pushing the metal aside; it is always visible from the back and gives a less sharply-defined but much more positive outline than engraving.

flatware Forks, spoons and other items of tableware that are generally flat, thus distinguished from hollow ware. Knives are cutlery, although the terms flatware and cutlery are often used interchangeably.

fluting Parallel concave grooves, the opposite of reeding.

gadrooning Similar decoration to beading, consisting of raised domes on a slant, originally derived from the knuckles of a clenched fist.

gauge Measure of the diameter of wire or thickness of sheet metal used in an article, referred to as heavy or light gauge according to its thickness.

German silver Not a silver at all but a combination of nickel, copper and zinc introduced to England by a German in the late 1700s. As its colour resembles silver, it makes the perfect base for silver-plated items. Also known as gunmetal, nickel silver, Argentan and Argentine.

gilding Process of overlaying or covering an article with a thin layer of gold or gold alloy either by melting gold with mercury and brushing it onto the surface before removing the mercury by evaporation under heat; by soaking a linen rag with a solution of chloride of gold, burning it and rubbing the ashes onto the silver; or by electrolysis.

gold Precious metal much used in jewellery; because pure gold is too soft, it is mixed with other metals, such as copper, silver, nickel and zinc to strengthen it; what and how much is added determines its colour and carat.

gold filled Technique of joining a thin layer of gold alloy to a base metal, indicated by the hallmark GF; a misleading term as the piece is not filled with gold.

gold plate Articles made of gold; a term often incorrectly applied to articles of gilded silver.

goldsmith Strictly, a worker in gold, although common usage also applies the term to a silversmith, and vice versa.

hallmark Strictly the punched marks on a silver, gold or platinum article to identify the hall (in London, the Goldsmiths' Hall, which oversaw the first assay marks in England, hence 'hallmark') or town assay office where the article was assayed; the term now includes the standard hallmark to attest the legally required purity of the metal, the maker's mark and the date mark.

hollow ware Vessels, jugs, pots, tankards, etc., as distinct from flat tableware.

inlay See **damascene**

loaded Item such as a hollow candlestick filled with pitch, resin or other heavy substance to give it stability; also known as filled.

lustre Appearance of a smooth surface of silver, gold and other minerals caused by light striking the surface, enhanced by polishing, buffing and burnishing.

maker's mark Mark punched on an item to indicate the maker, usually his or her initials.

matting Punching of dots to produce a rough surface.

milled Ground, fluted edge, for example on a coin.

moulding Border or soldered-on mount, cast or hammered, and sometimes pierced.

mount Bases, rims and handles of silver or gold mounted or added to wood, ceramics and glass items to cover raw edges and add decoration.

nickel silver Silver-white alloy of copper, nickel and zinc in varying proportions, usually 2:1:1 to 3:1:1.

niello Black alloy of silver, copper, lead and sulphur used to fill an engraving.

parcel-gilt Object that has been partially gilded.

patina Thin, greenish film or discolouration on bronze and copper caused by exposure to the atmosphere; by extension, the term now describes the reddish patina-effect on gold and the patina on silver caused by numerous shallow scratches.

pedestal foot Raised base of a vessel,

usually in stepped or classical shapes; originally used for stone columns.

pewter Alloy of tin with lead, antimony or, in the case of old pewter, copper; bismuth is sometimes added to harden the alloy.

pierced Decorative patterns once cut with punches, now stamped.

Pinchbeck Solid metal made by mixing copper and zinc, discovered by Christopher Pinchbeck (1670–1732); the name is often wrongly used for gold-filled or rolled gold-plated items.

pitch Thick, tarry resin, originally used to caulk ships; used for loading and for filling knife-handles.

planishing Technique of further hammering an object after raising, using a special tool that smooths out previous hammer marks and corrects any irregularities of thickness or shape.

plate British gold and silver objects; not to be confused with plated objects, which are electroplated.

plated or composite metal Two or more layers of different metals joined to each other by plating, without being fused together as an alloy.

plating Process of covering or overlaying a base metal or alloy with silver or gold either by close plating or electroplating.

platinum One of the heaviest, most durable and most valuable metals used in jewellery. The ore that yields platinum also contains palladium and rhodium, which are also used in jewellery.

precious or noble metals Silver, gold and platinum.

punched Decorative strengthening rows of raised beads formed by using a punch on the undersurface.

raising Method by which a saucer-shaped circle of silver or gold is hammered over cast-iron raising stakes to the desired shape, such as a bowl; frequent annealing is necessary to keep the metal evenly distributed, without bubbles, wrinkles or cracks.

reeding Parallel lines of convex decoration; the opposite of fluting.

repoussé Further improvement of embossed decoration by working punches from the front to vary degree, sharpen outline and provide background detail.

rolled gold plate Technique of joining a thick layer of gold alloy to a base metal, which is then drawn to the thickness required; indicated by the hallmark RGP.

Sheffield Plate Plated or composite metal made by fusing a thin silver plate onto a thicker base metal (usually copper) plate and then rolling it into sheets, the resulting metal retaining the original proportions throughout; invented by Thomas Boulsover of Sheffield in 1742 and developed commercially in the 1750s, although the term itself was not used until 1771. Sheffield Plate was largely superseded in the 1830s by British Plate and, in the 1840s, by the cheaper process of electroplating.

silver Precious metal refined to .999 pure and then mixed with other metals for strength; much used in jewellery and tableware.

silver depositing Technique of decorating the surface of a piece of glass or ceramic ware with silver by electroplating.

silver foil Paper-thin sheet of silver made by hammering sheet silver and used by beating it onto a metal object or securing it by means of a fixative. Silver leaf is even

thinner (usually 0.005 mm thick) and is made by hammering a silver sheet placed between copper plates or sheets of parchment. Both silver foil and silver leaf are too thin and fragile to be used satisfactorily in making silverware.
silver gilt Object made of silver and then gilded.
silver plate Articles made of silver; term often incorrectly applied to silver-plated or Sheffield Plate articles.
silver-plated Articles made of a base metal given a silver surface by means of close plating or electroplating; distinguished from items made from plated metal, such as Sheffield Plate.
silversmith Strictly, a worker in silver, although common usage also applies the term to a goldsmith, and vice versa.
silverware Collectively, articles of silver, Sheffield Plate and silver-plated ware.
single-plated Type of plated metal covered with a layer of silver on one side, used for articles in which the underside is not on view.
sinking Method by which a circle of sheet silver or gold is hammered over a hollow depression in the goldsmith's block until it is saucer-shaped.
solder Metal alloy, usually of silver and zinc, used in molten form to join two separately made parts of a piece together, the solder having a lower melting point than that of the metal pieces to be joined.
spinning Production of hollow wares on a spinning lathe by means of forcing a disc of silver up around a shaped wood block so that it takes its likeness.
stamping Mechanical production of parts in quantity, complete with decoration, by the use of hard steel dies, cut in reverse to the required pattern.
standard hallmark Hallmark stamped on a gold or silver article to attest the purity of the metal; the lion passant is currently used in England, the lion rampant in Scotland and the crowned harp in Ireland.
sterling Silver of the standard British value of purity (92.5%), assayed as such and then hallmarked.
strapwork Ribbon-type applied ornament; now used for any applied ornament.
tableware Items used to serve food at table, including plates, bowls, glasses, cutlery and flatware.
tarnish Blackish surface colour on silver caused by contact with sulphurous fumes or by a thin surface deposit; wrongly believed to be the result of oxidation.
tine Prong of a fork or tooth of a comb.
touch marks or touches Makers' marks applied to pewter objects.
turned Silverware made, decorated or finished on a lathe.
vermeil French term for items made of sterling silver gilded with gold.
wire drawing Method by which silver rod is drawn through ever-diminishing holes to the required thickness, down to a hair's breadth, achieved by constant annealing.
wirework Framework, decoration or supports of an article made of silver or plated silver wire.

2 Pewter and Sheffield Plate

This section looks at the quite different marks to be found on Old Sheffield Plate. A representative selection of pewter makers' marks is provided next, as an introduction to these once common household wares. Finally there is an examination of some traditional techniques used in working with precious metals.

Old Sheffield Plate

Old Sheffield Plate was manufactured for about 100 years. It was accidentally discovered in 1742 by Thomas Boulsover, who fused a thin layer of silver onto copper to make an appealing new product that looked like silver but cost a fraction of its price. He used it mainly for small objects such as buttons, snuff boxes and buckles. He tried to keep his process a secret, but it was soon copied and used for everything from candlesticks to teapots.

need to know

Sheffield Plate is always less expensive than silver but can command high prices when in good condition.

From about 1770 some pieces of Sheffield Plate with a visible interior, such as bowls, were made by the double sandwich method, in which silver was fused to each side of a sheet of copper.

A problem was soon discovered with Sheffield Plate, in that the silver would wear away and reveal the copper beneath. So from around 1760, a greater proportion of silver to copper was used, although precise standards varied greatly.

The manufacturers of Old Sheffield Plate were often also silversmiths, and all the makers followed popular styles of silverware for their designs. The demise of Old Sheffield Plate was brought about in the 1840s by a new process called British plate, which itself was replaced later in the century by the even cheaper electroplating process.

Marks on Old Sheffield Plate

There are a number of problems with identifying and dating Old Sheffield Plate by its marks. For instance, a precise date cannot be given, as the makers' marks appeared without the date letter that is struck on all solid silver. And, because of the resemblance they bore to silver marks, marks on Sheffield Plate were made illegal altogether in 1773. From 1784 marks were again permitted, but had to be easily distinguishable from silver marks. Some manufacturers ignored the new law and used marks looking quite similar to those on silver, some obeyed the letter of the law and others did not bother to use a mark at all.

From 1765 to 1825, the crown was used by some makers as a guarantee of quality. From 1820 some makers stamped an identification such as 'Best Sheffield Heavy Silver Plating' on their products.

Other guidelines

After 1835 electroplating often simulated Sheffield Plate, and later pieces are often passed off as Sheffield Plate even though made by a quite different process.

One reliable way of telling Old Sheffield Plate from its imitators is by its colour – it has a soft, slightly bluish glow. The old plating process meant that hollow objects had a seam on them, whereas electroplating covers a piece seamlessly.

The words 'Sheffield Plated' when marked on an object actually mean it has been electroplated – the opposite of what one would expect.

Something else to watch out for is the foreign competition: cheap French imports of far inferior quality. These are only lightly silvered and have a reddish glow, rather than the bluish one of the genuine article.

Makers' marks on Old Sheffield Plate

The makers' marks illustrated on pages 104–109 are a selection from the many that are to be found.

Key to abbreviations

B Birmingham
L London
N Nottingham
S Sheffield

need to know

Early Sheffield Plate makers applied a thin film of solder over the bare edge of copper. Such pieces are very rare.

Towards the end of the 18th century, a U-shaped section of silver wire was used to hide the copper edge; this can be felt as a lip on the underside and is a useful means of identification.

Most pieces of Sheffield Plate hollow ware, such as candlesticks, have a visible seam. If there is no seam, the piece has been replated or it is not Sheffield Plate.

Marks with full names A-H

1 Lea, Abner Cowel, 1808 **B**
2 Goodman, Alexander & Co., 1800 **S**
3 Allgood, John, 1812 **B**
4 Ashforth, G & Co., 1784 **S**
5 Ashley, 1816 **B**
6 Askew, 1828 **N**
7 Banister, William, 1808 **B**
8 Barnet
9 Beldon, George, 1809 **S**
10 Beldon, Hoyland & Co. 1785 **S**
11 Best, Henry, 1814 **B**
12 Best & Wastidge, 1816 **S**
13 Bishop, Thomas, 1830
14 Boulton, 1784 **B**
15 Bradshaw, Joseph, 1822 **B**
16 Brittain, Wilkinson & Brownill, 1785 **S**
17 Butts, T, 1807 **B**
18 Causer, John Fletcher, 1824 **B**
19 Cheston, Thomas, 1809 **B**
20 Child, Thomas, 1821 **B**
21 Needham, C. 1821 **S**
22 Cope, Charles Gretter, 1817 **B**

23 Corn, James & Sheppard, John, 1819 **B**
24 Cracknall, John, 1814 **B**
25 Creswick, Thomas & James, 1811 **S**
26 Holy, Daniel, Parker & Co. 1804 **S**

1 

2 

3 

4 ASHFORTH & CO

5 

6 ASKEW MAKER NOTTINGHAM

7 

8 BARNET

9 

10 

11 

12 

13 

14 

15 

16 

17 BUTTS

18 CAUSER

19 

20 CHILD

21 C NEEDHAM MAKER SHEFFIELD

22 

23 CORN & Cº

24 

25 CRESWICKS

26 

Marks with full names H

1 Holy, Daniel, Wilkinson & Co., 1784 **S**
2 Davis, John, 1816 **B**
3 Horton, David, 1808 **B**
4 Deakin, Smith & Co., 1785 **S**
5 Dixon & Co., 1784 **B**
6 Dunn, G B, 1810 **B**
7 Goodwin, Edward, 1794 **S**
8 Ellerby, W, 1803
9 Moore, F, 1820 **B**
10 Fox, Proctor Pasmore & Co., 1784 **S**
11 Freeth, Henry, 1784 **S**
12 Froggatt, Coldwell & Lean, 1797 **S**
13 Gainsford, Robert, 1808 **S**
14 Garnett, William, 1803 **S**
15 Gibbs, Joseph, 1808 **B**
16 Gilbert, John, 1812 **B**
17 Green, Joseph, 1807 **B**
18 Hall, William, 1820 **B**
19 Hancock, Joseph, 1755 **S**
20 Hanson, Matthias, 1810 **B**
21 Harrison, Joseph, 1809 **B**
22 Harwood, T, 1816
23 Hatfield, Aaron, 1808 **S**
24 Hatfield, Aaron, 1810 **S**
25 Hill, Daniel & Co., 1806 **B**
26 Hinks, Joseph, 1812 **B**
27 Hipkiss, J, 1808 **B**
28 Hobday, J, 1829

Marks with full names H-M

1 Holland, H & Co., 1784 **B**
2 Horton, John, 1809 **B**
3 Howard, Stanley & Thomas, 1809 **L**
4 Hutton, William, 1807 **B**
5 Wilkinson, Henry & Co., 1836 **S**
6 Drabble, James & Co., 1805 **S**
7 Green, John & Co., 1799 **S**
8 Love, John & Co., 1785 **S**
9 Roberts, J & S, 1786 **S**
10 Waterhouse, J & Co., 1833 **S**
11 Dixon, James & Son, 1835 **S**
12 Linwood, John, 1807 **B**
13 Nicholds, James, 1808 **B**
14 Jones, 1824 **B**
15 Parsons, John & Co., 1784 **S**
16 Johnson, James, 1812 **B**
17 Jordan, Thomas, 1814 **B**
18 Lilly, Joseph, 1816 **B**
19 Kirkby, Samuel, 1812 **S**
20 Law, Thomas, 1758 **S**
21 Law, John & Son, 1807 **S**
22 Lees, George, 1811 **B**
23 Lees, George, 1811 **B**
24 Lilly, John, 1815 **B**
25 Linwood, John, 1807 **B**
26 Linwood, Matthew & Son, 1808 **B**
27 Love, Silverside, Darby & Co., 1785 **S**
28 Mappin Bros, 1850

1 

2 HOR TON

3 How ard

4 Hutton

5 H·WILKINSON&C°

6 I·DRABBLE &C°

7 I GREEN&C°

8 I LOVE &C°

9 I&S. ROBERTS.

10 I&I WATERHOUSE&C°

11 J DIXON

12 J. LIN WOOD

13 J·NICHOLDS

14 JOHN·PARSONS&C°

15 JONES

16 JOHN SON

17 JOR DAN

18 JOS·H·LILLY

19 KIRKBY· FOR·USE

20 LAW

21 LAW&SON

22 LEES

23 Lees

24 LILLY

25 LINWOOD

26 

27 LOVE SILVERSIDE DARBY &C°

28 

Marks with full names M-S

1 Meredith, Henry, 1807 **B**
2 Moore, Frederick, 1820 **B**
3 Morton, Richard & Co., 1785 **S**
4 Smith, N & Co., 1784 **S**
5 Peake, 1807 **B**
6 Pearson, Richard, 1811 **B**
7 Pemberton & Mitchell, 1817 **B**
8 Pimley, Samuel, 1810 **B**
9 Madin, P & Co., 1788 **S**
10 Prime, J, 1839
11 Law, Richard, 1807 **B**
12 Roberts & Cadman, 1785 **S**
13 Rodgers, Joseph & Sons, 1822 **S**
14 Rogers, John, 1819 **B**
15 Ryland, William & Sons, 1807 **B**
16 Sansom, Thomas & Sons. 1821 **S**
17 Scot, William, 1807 **B**
18 Younge, S & C & Co., 1813 **S**
19 Colmore, S, 1790 **S**
20 Evans, Samuel, 1816 **B**
21 Shepard, Joseph, 1817 **B**
22 Silk, Robert, 1809 **B**
23 Silkirk, William, 1807 **B**
24 Small, Thomas, 1812 **B**
25 Smith, Isaac, 1821 **B**
26 Smith, William, 1812 **B**
27 Smith & Co., 1784 **B**
28 Staniforth, Parkin & Co., 1784 **S**

Marks with full names S-W

1 Stot, Benjamin, 1811 **S**
2 Turley, Samuel, 1816 **B**
3 Sykes & Co., 1784 **S**
4 Worton, Samuel, 1821 **B**
5 Thomas, Stephen, 1813 **B**
6 Thomason, Edward & Dowler, 1807 **B**
7 Law, Thomas & Co., 1784 **S**
8 Tonks, Samuel, 1807 **B**
9 Tonks & Co., 1824 **B**
10 Tudor & Co., 1784 **S**
11 Turton, John, 1820 **B**
12 Tyndall, Joseph, 1813 **B**
13 Waterhouse & Co., 1807 **B**
14 Waterhouse, Hatfield & Co., 1836 **S**
15 Watson, Fenton & Bradbury, 1795 **S**
16 Watson, Pass & Co., 1811 **S**
17 Watson, W, 1833 **S**
18 Bingley, William, 1787 **B**
19 Coldwell, William, 1806 **S**
20 Green, W & Co., 1784 **S**
21 Hipwood, William, 1809 **B**
22 White, John, 1811 **B**
23 Willmore, Joseph, 1807 **B**
24 Jervis, William, 1789 **S**
25 Linwood, William, 1807 **B**
26 Markland, William, 1818 **B**
27 Newbould, William & Sons, 1804 **S**
28 Woodward, William, 1814 **B**
29 Wright & Fairbairn, 1809 **S**

1 

2 

3 

4 

5 

6 

7 

8 

9 

10 

11  

12 

13 

14 

15 

16 

17 W WATSON
MAKER
SHEFFIELD

18 

19 

20 

21 

22 

23 WILLMORE

24 

25  

26 W MARKLAND

27 

28 

29 

Marks with initials only

13 

14 

15 

16 

18 

22 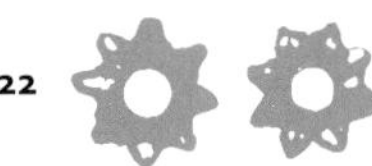

23 

24 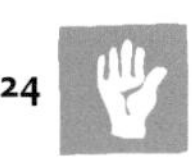

25 

26  

27 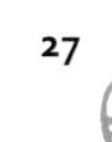 

28 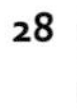 

1 Ashforth, Ellis & Co., 1770 **S**
2 Hatfield, Aaron, 1808 **S**
3 Boulton & Fothergill, 1764 **S**
4 Atkin, Henry, 1833
5 Tudor & Leader, 1760 **S**
6 Tudor & Leader, 1760 **S**
7 Hancock, Joseph, 1755 **S**
8 Littlewood, J, 1772 **S**
9 Rowbotham, J & Co., 1768 **S**
10 Winter, John & Co., 1765 **S**
11 Hoyland, John & Co., 1764 **S**
12 Smallwood, J, 1823
13 Hoyland, John & Co., 1764 **S**
14 Roberts, Jacob & Samuel, 1765 **S**
15 Morton, Richard, 1765 **S**
16 Morton, Richard, 1765 **S**
17 Smith, Nathaniel, 1756 **S**
18 Roberts & Briggs, 1860
19 Butts, T, 1807
20 Briggs, W, 1823
21 Hutton, W, 1849

MARKS USING SYMBOLS ONLY

22 Boulton, M & Co., 1784 **S**
23 Fenton, Matthew & Co., 760 **S**
24 Watson, J & Son, 1830, Or Padley, Parkin & Co., 1849
25 Smith, Sissons & Co., 1848
26 Tudor & Leader, 1760 **S**
27 Blagden, Hodgson & Co., 1821
28 Walker, Knowles & Co., 1840

Pewter

Pewter is an alloy of tin with lead, antimony or (notably in the case of fine old pewter) copper. Sometimes bismuth is added to harden the alloy. The proportions of the various metals in the alloy vary greatly, but generally speaking, the more tin, the better the pewter. Britannia metal is similar, and is of high quality, being mostly tin with a small amount of antimony and copper.

need to know

The Pewterers' Company regulated the quality of the alloy, in much the same way as the Goldsmiths' Company assayed silver and gold.

Pewter-making began in the Middle Ages; pewter plates replaced wooden ones, and remained popular until superseded by china in the 19th century. A vast amount of domestic pewterware was produced in Britain. Pewter in Britain usually imitated silverware. Often damaged in use, and of low perceived value, much has been lost.

Reproduction pewter has been made since the 1920s, including Liberty's Art Nouveau 'Tudric' range; now quite collectable. However, most collectors prefer antique pewter, with its superior patina and finish. It is the marks on antique pewter that are covered here.

Standards of pewter

The three principal types of pewter are:

- Ley pewter: 80% tin, 20% lead
- Trifle pewter: 82% or 83% tin, 17% or 18% antimony
- Plate pewter: 86% tin, 7% antimony, 3.5% copper, 3.5% bismuth

Quality marks

Ley and trifle pewter did not carry any marks of quality. Plate pewter was marked with a letter 'X', sometimes with a crown above it (**1**), or was stamped with the words 'hard metal' or 'superfine hard metal'

1 2

3

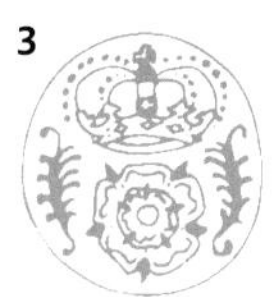

(**2**). A rose and crown stamp (**3**) also indicated fine quality pewter. At first for export ware only, by the 18th century this mark was more generally used. From the late 17th century, the word 'London' was added, but is no guarantee of provenance.

Touch marks

By far the most important marks on pewter are the 'touch marks' or 'touches'. These identify the maker, and take their name from official 'touchplates' on which they were stamped at Pewterers' Hall. A maker's touch mark might be simply his initials or name, but could also incorporate elaborate designs. Dates also occasionally form part of the mark, but indicate the year registered, not the year a piece was made.

Other marks

Good early pewter often bears elaborate ownership marks in a raised form, rather like a wax seal.

Small marks are also found on pewter similar to silver hallmarks, usually consisting of four shields (**1**). The symbols in the shields deceptively followed genuine silver marks quite closely.

After 1826, tankards and measures used in taverns had to carry capacity marks. These were of local design until 1877, after which they were validated by an excise mark consisting of a crown over the monarch's initials and a code number, denoting the area where the inspection of capacity had been carried out (**2**).

Sample touch marks

The touch marks shown on pages 112–113 are a small selection of examples where identification of the maker is possible. They are taken from touchplates I and IV at Pewterers' Hall, and illustrate the variety that exists among the touch marks registered there. If the touch mark you are seeking is not included, you should consult a specialist reference work on pewter marks.

Note that 'master', 'warden', 'steward' and 'yeoman' were ranks within the Pewterers' Company.

need to know

The earliest touchplates dated from the beginning of the 15th century but were lost in the Great Fire of London in 1666. The practice of registering marks on the touchplates began again two years later and continued until 1824.

The marks do not appear on the touchplates in chronological order, having been punched in any empty space in a haphazard fashion. Five copper touchplates survive at the Pewterers' Company, but the corresponding register of makers has been lost, making individual identification impossible in many cases.

The size of the touch marks varies according to the size of the item on which they appear, but as a very general rule, early marks tend to be smaller than later ones.

1

2

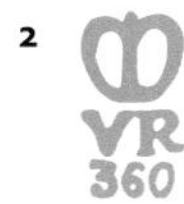

Sample marks from touchplate I

1 'RL' in an oval with a comet between the letters. Robert Lucas, who became a steward of the Pewterers' Company in 1651 and master in 1667.

2 'NK' in a beaded circle with a hand grasping a rose. Thought to be Nicholas Kelk, master in 1665, 1681 and 1686.

3 SI' in a small beaded circle with a lamb and flag. Probably Samuel Jackson, working in the late 17th c.

4 'WA' in a small circle. Possibly William Austin or William Ayliffe, both working in the late 17th c.

5 'TF' in a beaded oval with a fountain. This is a pun on the maker's name, Thomas Fontaine or Fountain, who took up his livery in 1670.

6 'William Burton' in a beaded circle with a hand holding a sceptre. He was a warden in 1675 and 1680, and master in 1685.

7 'RH' in a beaded circle with a locust, three stars and the date [16]56. Ralph Hulls, warden in 1671 and 1677, master in 1682.

8 'C' in a beaded circle with a crown and cockerel. Another play on a name – Humphrey Cock, who took up his livery in 1679.

9 'John Bull' with a bull's head and two stars in a beaded circle. Late 17th c.

10 'PP' in a circle with a beacon and the date 1668. This could be the mark of Peter Parke or Peter Priest.

11 'SA' in a beaded circle with a lion rampant. Thought to be Sam Atley, who took his livery in 1667.

12 'SQ' in a beaded heart with an arrow and a key with the date [16]73. Thought to be Sam Quissenborough.

Sample marks from touchplate IV

1 'Henry Maxted' with pillars and the Sun shining on a rose. Yeoman 1731.

2 'John Kenrick' with a stork between two pillars. Yeoman 1737, warden 1754.

3 'Philip Roberts' with a lion rampant and a crescent. Yeoman 1738.

4 'RC' in a beaded circle with a lamb holding a crook. Thought to be a play on the name Robert Crooke. Yeoman 1738.

5 'I Perry' with a female figure between pillars. Yeoman 1743, warden 1773.

6 'Iohn Hartwell' with a saltire and four castles. Yeoman 1736.

7 'Ionathan Leach' with a quartered shield of arms showing a rose, a sprig of laurel and a lamb and flag. The fourth quarter is illegible. Yeoman 1732.

8 'Thomas Giffin' with a dagger piercing a heart and a ducal coronet, all between pillars. Yeoman 1759.

9 'A Jenner' in a plain rectangle. Thought to be Anthony Jenner, yeoman 1754.

10 'Jno Appleton' with a still and a worm. Yeoman 1768, warden 1799, master 1800.

11 'C Swift' in an indented square with a thistle and a rose. Yeoman 1770.

12 'Wood & Hill' with two sheep in a shield. Thought to be Thomas Wood (Yeoman 1792) and Roger Hill (Yeoman 1791).

Note: 'I' was often used for 'J'. 'Ino' and 'Jno' stand for 'John'.

Precious metal working

The surface of metal can be textured by cutting or scoring it with sharp tools, by stamping it with patterned punches, by etching it with acid, and by applying extra pieces of metal. Variations in texture produce subtle changes of light reflection and diffraction. These are some of the most common techniques and tools.

Tools and techniques

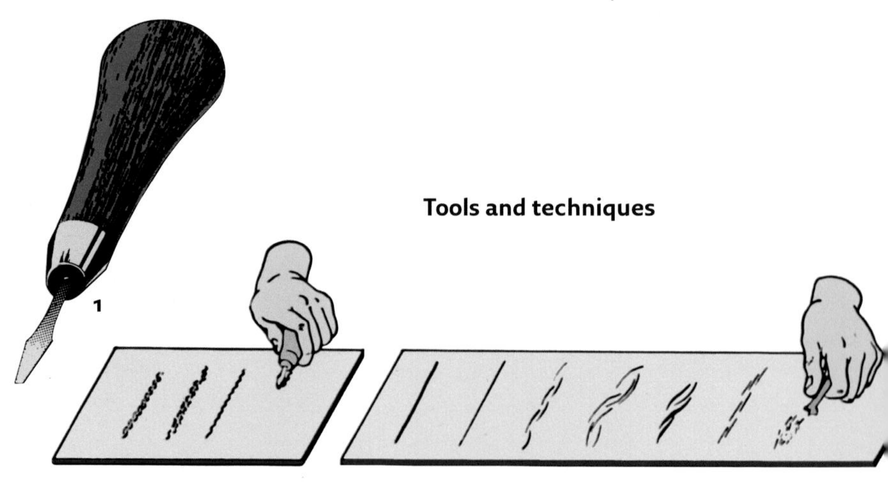

1 Wiggle engraver

A wiggle engraver is gripped firmly in the hand and moved from side to side through the metal. This makes a wiggly line.

2, 3, 4 Chasing punches

Chasing punches are struck into the metal with a hammer so that their pattern is transferred to the metal surface.

5 Scorper

A very sharp tool with a blade made of tempered steel. It is gripped so that the thumb lies along the blade and can be used to guide the stroke. Variations in the line can be achieved by altering the

Engraved silver beaker from Holland, 17th century

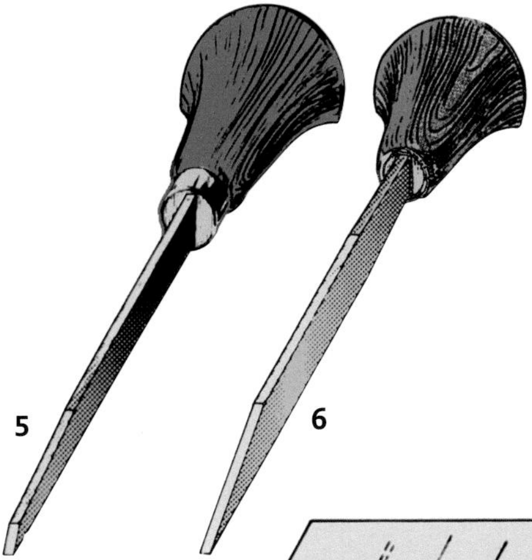

5

6

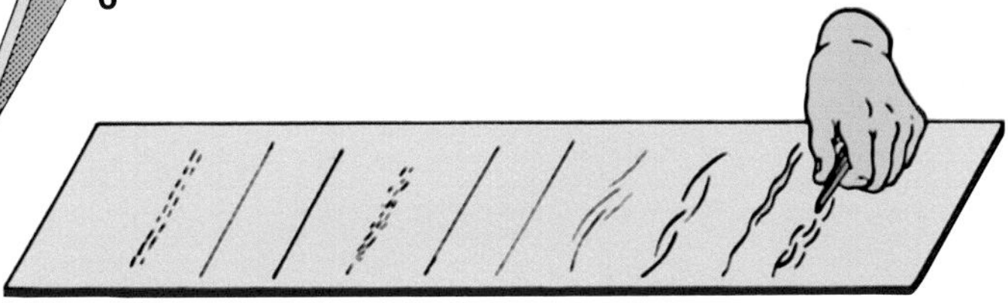

pressure on the tool, or by changing the angle of the tool against the metal.

6 Graver

Used to cut long flowing lines on the metal, or short marks for a rough texture. As with the scorpers, the line can be varied by altering hand pressure or the angle of the tool.

7 Vibro-engraver

Used with various patterns of head to produce lines of varying quality. The head vibrates so that it cuts into the metal; the operator guides the tool so that it produces lines or areas of texture.

Damascene work

Damascene inlay is done by hammering the inlay metal into gouged recesses.

a The pattern to be damascened is drawn out onto the metal, and a sharp graver or scorper is used to cut away the metal in the pattern areas. At the edges of each incision the craftsman undercuts the ground metal slightly to provide purchase for the inlay metal.

b The inlay metal is placed in the recesses and hammered into the grooves so that it spreads into the undercuts and is secured. The entire surface is then smoothed and polished.

Damascene inlay on Moghul daggers

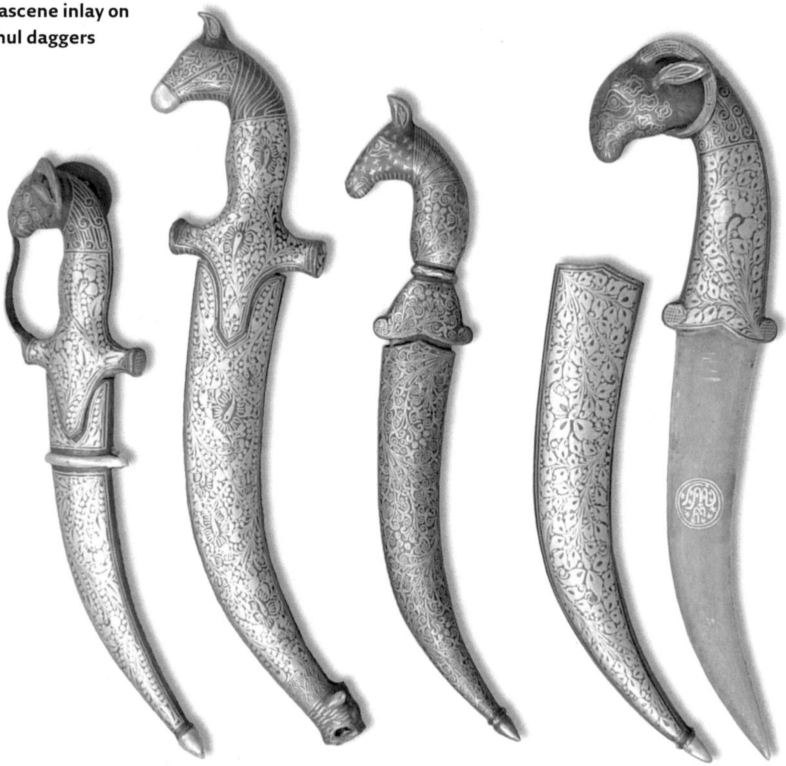

Native American punch tools

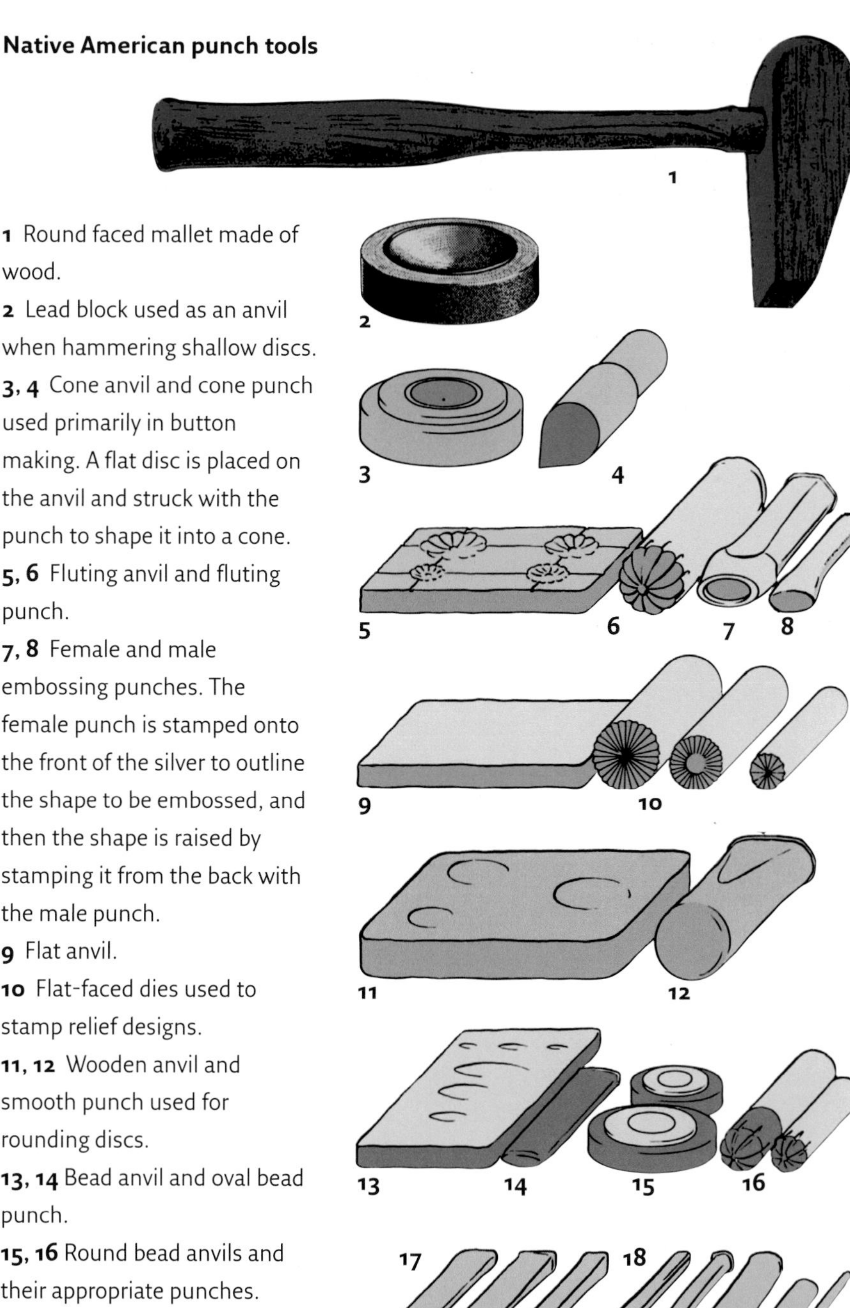

1 Round faced mallet made of wood.

2 Lead block used as an anvil when hammering shallow discs.

3, 4 Cone anvil and cone punch used primarily in button making. A flat disc is placed on the anvil and struck with the punch to shape it into a cone.

5, 6 Fluting anvil and fluting punch.

7, 8 Female and male embossing punches. The female punch is stamped onto the front of the silver to outline the shape to be embossed, and then the shape is raised by stamping it from the back with the male punch.

9 Flat anvil.

10 Flat-faced dies used to stamp relief designs.

11, 12 Wooden anvil and smooth punch used for rounding discs.

13, 14 Bead anvil and oval bead punch.

15, 16 Round bead anvils and their appropriate punches.

17 Scalloping punches.

18 Detail punches.

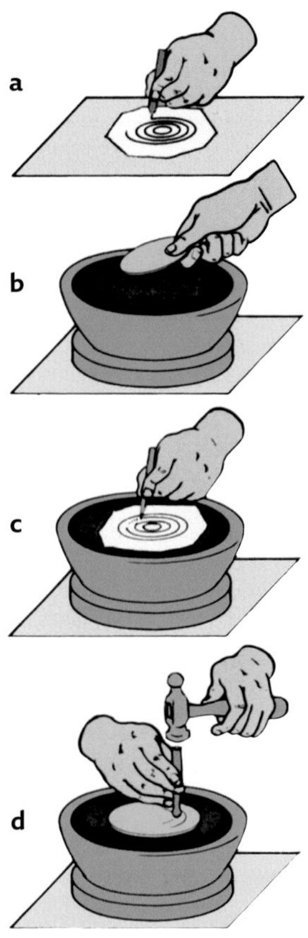

Repoussé work

Repoussé is a French word meaning "pushed back". The process involves pressing or striking the reverse surface of the metal so that a design appears on the front.

a The design is drawn out on a piece of thin paper the same size as the metal.

b The metal is placed on a pitch bowl and warmed slightly. The warming makes the metal adhere to the pitch so that it will not move during the work, and it also makes the metal a little more malleable.

c The drawing is placed on top of the metal, and the lines of the design are traced with a stylus.

d The paper is removed and the design is pressed into the metal, using repoussé punches and chasing punches. When the design has been made on the metal it is removed from the pitch bowl, and the front of the design is tidied up by levelling the areas between the raised parts of the pattern. It is then returned to the pitch bowl face down, and the final touching up of the design is done with the punches.

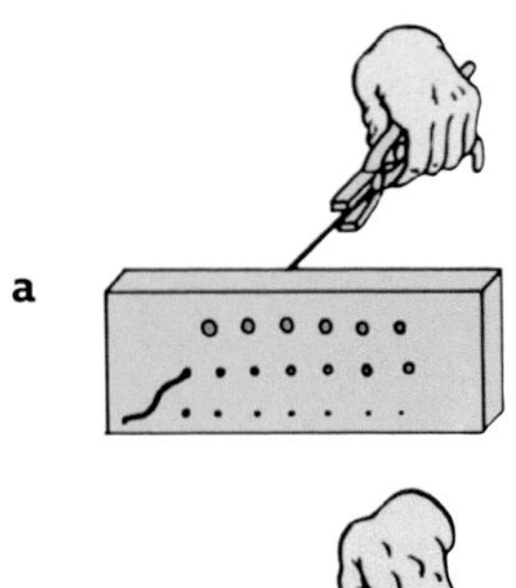

Chain making

Chain making is a precise process, and care is needed to ensure that all the links are of even thickness and size.

a Wire of the required thickness is drawn through a drawplate.

b The wire is wound in a spiral around a former. The shape of the former will determine the shape of the links.

c The spiral of metal is sawn through on one side; this produces numerous pieces of curved wire that are all the same length and curved to the same shape.
d The pieces of wire can then be interlocked. The two ends of each link are aligned and pinched together firmly with pliers so that they will not come apart, and then soldered.

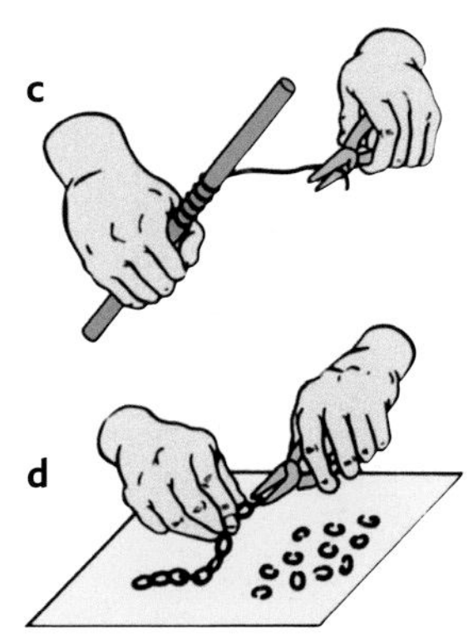

Pierced work

Pierced work involves drilling holes in the metal so that the saw blade can be threaded through.
a A centre punch is used to mark a small impression on the metal so that the drill bit will not slip. A drop of oil is added for lubrication.
b A hole big enough to take the blade of the piercing saw is drilled through the metal within the outline of the perspective hole.
c The saw blade is threaded through, teeth downward, and attached to the saw frame. The outline of the pierced work can now be traced with the saw cut; this process is repeated with every part of the metal to be pierced.
d When the pierced work is completed, the sawn edges are filed and polished to smooth and finish them.

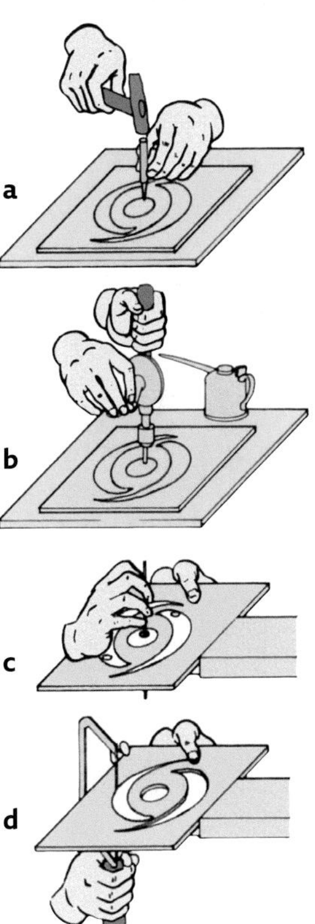

a

b

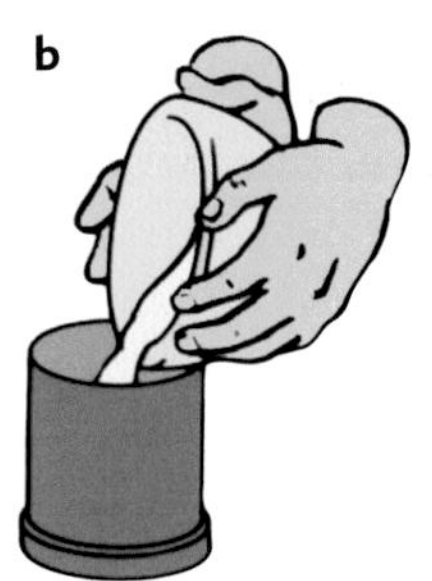

c

d

e

f

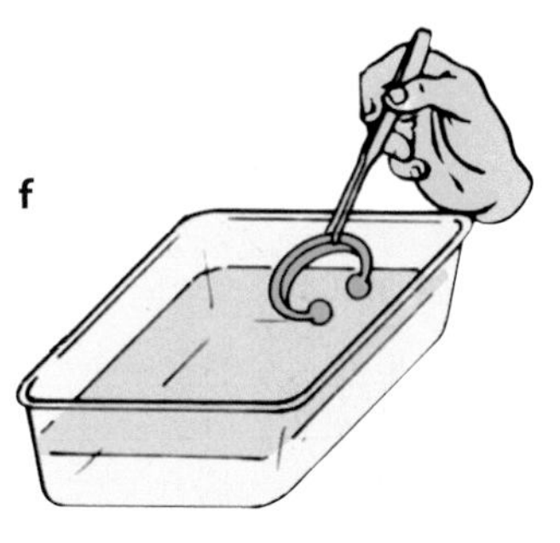

Investing and casting

Investing is the process of creating a mould around the original model.

a The investment powder is mixed with water to the correct creamy consistency.

b The model to be invested is attached via a wax cone to a sprue base; a flask is fitted to the base and filled with investment mix.

Casting is the process of filling the cavity in the mould with molten metal to produce a finished piece.

c The metal that is to be cast is melted in a crucible until it is red hot. Any impurities are removed from the surface of the metal so that they will not marr the casting.

d The metal is poured into the cavity in the mould, and allowed to set.

e When the metal is cool, the mould is broken and chipped away from the casting. The sprues that carried the molten metal to the casting are snipped off with sprue cutters.

f The casting is placed in an acid bath and scrubbed with wire brushes to clean away all traces of the mould material. When the casting is properly clean it can be buffed and polished in the manner suitable to the metal.

Filigree work

Filigree is a technique that involves forming patterns from bent and twisted wire, either on a background or as a latticework.

a The pattern to be interpreted in filigree work is drawn onto a piece of paper, and wires of the chosen type are twisted and coiled into flat shapes that correspond to the design.

b When all the parts of the design have been laid out in wire, the sections of wire are carefully soldered together at the point where they touch.

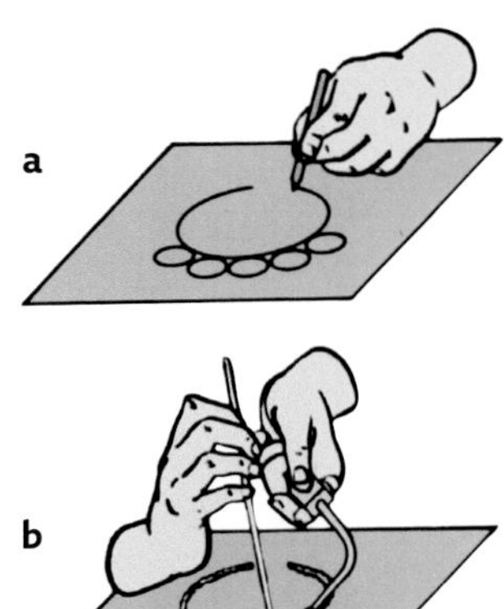

Chenier work

Chenier is the name given to decorative wire tubing; the process of making chenier is similar to that of wiredrawing, though slightly more complicated.

a A strip is cut out of metal plate, and one end is tapered slightly so that it will slip easily into the drawplate.

b The strip of metal is placed over a half-round former, and a metal or wood rod is hammered over the top to force the metal into the channel.

c The curved shape is put through an appropriate hole in a drawplate, and is pulled through the plate with tongs. This forms it virtually into a circle.

d The tube is then drawn through a joint tool, with the seam towards the top. The screw of the joint firms and smooths the join in the chenier, and the tube is now fully circular.

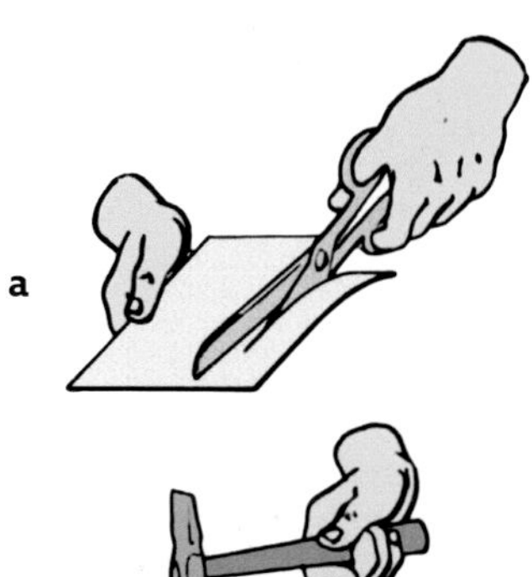

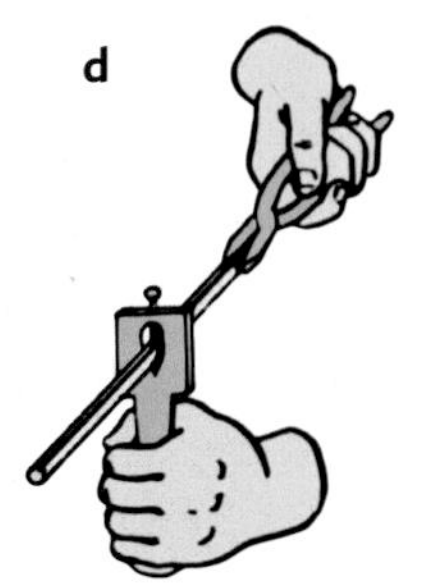

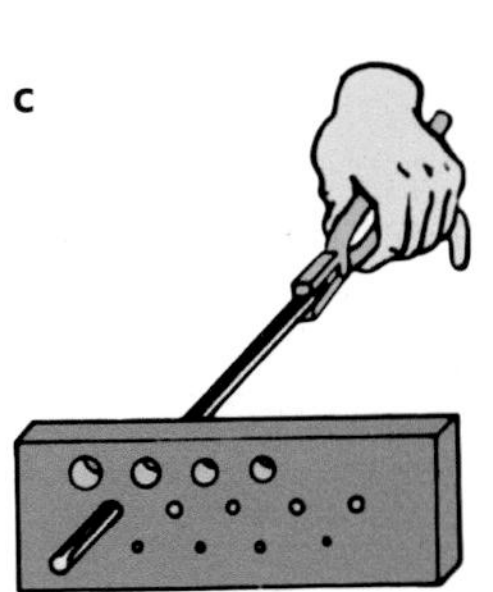

3 Ceramics

This section surveys the vast range of marks to be found on pottery or porcelain, both from Britain and the rest of Europe, and from China and Japan. There are also profiles of leading pottery and porcelain manufacturers, some background information on methods of ceramic construction and surface work, and a glossary of ceramic terminology.

Pottery and porcelain

Unlike the strictly regulated hallmarks which appear on precious metals – and which give today's collector a foolproof means of identification – the marks that appear on pottery and porcelain are a far from reliable guide to provenance.

Marks may be blurred and impossible to identify. A particular mark can indicate a wide variety of periods and origins and the weight, colour, shape and pattern of the piece itself are a more reliable guide. The size and colour of the mark, and the way it was made, also have a bearing on its identification. Marks may also have been added fraudulently at or after manufacture.

Much pottery from every period bears no mark at all. A mark may refer to a factory, to a potter or painter who worked there, or to a past owner of the piece. Dates, too, are not to be taken at face value: when incorporated into a mark, they often indicate when the factory was established, or when a particular design was introduced. However, design registration marks were applied from 1842 to British wares and are a reliable guide, as are the date marks of Sèvres, Derby, Minton and Wedgwood.

The more you look at and handle pottery and porcelain, the more of a feel you will get for them. Only when you are very familiar with the wares themselves can marks be used as a back-up.

Chelsea soft-paste dwarf figurine, c. 1745

Pottery types

Pottery is made simply of clay, but with many additions to give added strength, and decorative glazes have been applied to enhance appearance. The following types are both common and important:

- **Creamware:** earthenware with a cream-coloured glaze, giving an impression of porcelain.
- **Delft:** Earthenware with a tin glaze, made in the 17th and 18th centuries.
- **Faïence:** Tin-glazed earthenware.
- **Majolica:** Decorative tin-glazed ware first made in 15th-century Italy and copied in the 19th century.
- **Stoneware:** A strong non-porous ware made from adding sand or flint to the clay.
- **Ironstone:** Patented by Mason in 1813, using slag from iron furnaces to strengthen the wares.

must know

When porcelain was first imported in the 15th century, it was a huge success in Europe and there were many attempts to reproduce it. The ingredients for the hard paste porcelain of the Chinese original were eventually found at Meissen in what is now Germany, and porcelain production began there in the early 18th century and soon afterwards throughout Europe.

Porcelain types

Porcelain was first made in China from china clay mixed with rock. It is noted for its strength, musical note when struck, and translucency.

Soft-paste porcelain, has a less hard, glittery glaze than hard-paste porcelain and less strength.

METHODS OF APPLYING MARKS

How a mark is made (and its colour) can help attribute it. There are four main methods:

- **Incising:** One of the earliest and simplest methods, a mark is scratched into the unfired clay.
- **Impressing:** A stamp is used to press a mark into the unfired clay.
- **Underglaze painting or transfer-printing:** Until 1850 this appeared only in blue, after which other colours were used. The mark was made before the final glaze was applied over it.
- **Overglaze marks:** These may be painted, transfer-printed or stencilled onto finished wares. They are easy for forgers to imitate.

Mark layout 1842-67

class (for pots)
year
month
day
bundle

Year codes 1842-67

A	1845	N	1864
B	1858	O	1862
C	1844	P	1851
D	1852	Q	1866
E	1855	R	1861
F	1847	S	1849
G	1863	T	1867
H	1843	U	1848
I	1846	V	1850
J	1854	W	1865
K	1857	X	1842
L	1856	Y	1853
M	1859	Z	1860

Mark layout 1868-83

class (for pots)
day
bundle
year
month

Year codes 1868-83

A	1871	K	1883
C	1870	L	1882
D	1878	P	1877
E	1881	S	1875
F	1873	U	1874
H	1869	V	1876
I	1872	X	1868
J	1880	Y	1879

Registered design marks

The system of Registered Designs was devised in 1839 to protect the design of industrial products in much the same way that the patent laws protect inventions. There were two early layouts of Registered Design Marks, one in use from 1842 to 1867, the other from 1868 to 1883

Month codes 1842-83

The same system of code letters was used to indicate the month of registration on both types of design mark layout shown above.

A	December	H	April
B	October	I	July
C/O	January	K	November
D	September	M	June
E	May	R	August
G	February	W	March

Registration numbers

From 1884, the complex diamond-shaped registration mark was replaced by a simple registration numbering system. The abbreviation 'Rd No' (for Registered Number) often appeared before the number. The system remains in use today. The dates of numbers used in the early years are given in the table below.

Rd No	Year	Rd No	Year	Rd No	Year
1	1884	205240	1893	385088	1902
19754	1885	224720	1894	402913	1903
40480	1886	246975	1895	425017	1904
64520	1887	268392	1896	447548	1905
90483	1888	291241	1897	471486	1906
116648	1889	311658	1898	493487	1907
141273	1890	331707	1899	518415	1908
163767	1891	351202	1900	534963	1909
185713	1892	368154	1901		

Ceramic makers' marks: A–Z

1 Paris, France. Painted red/gold, c. 1795

2 Bow, London, England. Red, c. 1765

3 Sèvres, France. Mark and date letter for 1753. Date letters ran alphabetically until 1793 (AA from 1778) appearing inside or alongside the 'crossed Ls' in blue (or later red) enamel

4 Sèvres, France, 1778

5 Nymphenberg, Germany. Impressed or incised, c. 1745

6 Arras, France. Soft-paste porcelain, 1770–90

7 'De Ster' (The Star), artist A Kiell. Delft, Holland, c. 1763

8 Helene Wolfsohn, decorator. Meissen, Germany, c. 1860

9 Meissen, Germany. Painted underglaze blue, c. 1725

10 Thomas Allen (painter). Wedgwood, 1875–1905

11 Burslem, Staffordshire, England. Impressed, c. 1750

12 Adams & Co, Tunstall, England, from c. 1790

13 New Jersey, USA. Printed, mid-19th c

14 Capo-di-Monte, Italy. Incised, c. 1760

15 Cartwright Bros, East Liverpool, Ohio, USA, 1880–1900

B

1 Flight & Barr, Worcester, England. Scratched in clay, 1793–1800. The most common Worcester marks are crescents, the letter W and copies of Chinese and Meissen marks

2 Worcester. Printed, 1807–13. Later Worcester wares carry the full name

3 Lille, France. Faïence, 1720–88

4 Bristol, England. Painted, c. 1773

5 Sèvres, France, 1754

6 Bristol, England, 1773

7 Bing & Grondahl, Copenhagen, Denmark, 1853

8 Knoller, Bayreuth, Germany. Faïence, c. 1730

9 Limbach, Germany. Porcelain, late 18th c

10 Niderviller, France, 1744–80

11 Barker, Sutton & Till, Burslem, Staffordshire, England, 1830–50

12 Belper Pottery, Derbyshire, England. Stoneware, 1812

13 'De Vergulde Bloompot' (The Golden Flowerpot), Delft, Holland, c. 1693

14 Enoch Booth, Tunstall, Staffordshire, England. Impressed, c. 1750

15 Bristol, England. Porcelain, c. 1750.

C

1 Nantes, France, c. 1780.
2-6 Caughley, England. Variations of the Caughley mark, printed or painted in underglaze blue, 1772–95
7 Bayreuth, Germany. Painted, 1744
8 Castel-Durante, Italy, c. 1570
9 'De Ster' (The Star), C D Berg, Delft, Holland, c. 1720
10 Coalport, Coalbrookdale, England. Hard-paste porcelain. Painted blue, c. 1825–50
11 Limoges, France. Hard-paste porcelain, c. 1783
12 Coalport, Coalbrookdale, England. Hard-paste porcelain. Painted blue, early 19th c
13 Leeds, England, c. 1760
14 St Cloud, France. Faïence/porcelain, c. 1711
15 Chelsea, London, England. Soft-paste porcelain, c. 1745
16 Worcester, England. Red, 1788–1808

D

1 Davenport, England. Impressed, 1793–1882
2 Derby, England, 1770–84
3 Caughley, England. Hard-paste porcelain. Painted blue, c. 1750
4 Derby, England. Soft-paste porcelain. Red, c. 1756
5 John Donaldson (painter), Worcester, England. Porcelain, c. 1770
6 Derby (Chelsea), England, c. 1782
7 Coalport, Coalbrookdale, England. Painted blue, c. 1825–50
8 William Littler, potter, Longton Hall, Staffordshire, England, 1750–60
9 Louis Dorez, Nord, France, c. 1735
10 Proskau, Silesia, Germany. Faïence, 1770–83
11 'De Paeuw' (The Peacock), Delft, Holland. Faïence, c. 1700
12 Derby, England. Incised, c. 1750
13 Limoges, France, c. 1875
14 Castleford, England. Pottery. Impressed, c. 1790
15 J van Duyn, 'De Porceleyne Schootel' (The Porcelain Dish), Delft, Holland. Faïence. Painted blue, c. 1764.

E

1 Elton Pottery, Somerset, England, 1880–90
2 St Petersburg, Russia, 1762–96
3 Derby, England, 1779
4 Paris, France, c. 1800
5 Moustiers, France. Faïence, 18th c
6 Hanley, England. Impressed, 18th c
7 Bow, London, England, c. 1754
8 Michael Edkins and his wife, Bristol, England. Blue, c. 1760
9 Henri Borne, Nevers, France, c. 1689
10 From 1891, the word 'England' appeared on English wares
11 Tunstall, Staffordshire, England, c. 1757
12 Burslem, England. Impressed, moulded or incised, 1784–90
13 Bennington, Vermont, USA. Impressed, c. 1882
14 Ernst Teichert, Meissen, Germany, late 19th c
15 E Jacquemin, Fontainebleau, France, 1862–66

F

1 Rouen, France. Faïence, c. 1644

2–3 Variations of mark of Furstenberg, Germany, 1760–70

4 Jacob Fortling, Copenhagen, Denmark. Faïence, 1755–62

5–6 Variations of mark of Bow, London, 1750–59

7 François Boussemart, Lille, France, c. 1750

8 Flight, Barr & Barr, Worcester, 1813–40

9 Rouen, France, 1673–96

10 Buen Retiro, Madrid, Spain. Soft-paste porcelain, c. 1759

11 Turin, Italy. Faïence, 16th c

12 Flight & Barr, Worcester, England, 1792–1807

13–14 Variations of Worcester Flight marks, 1782–91

15 Bordeaux, France, 1781–87

16 Fulper Bros, Flemington, New Jersey, USA. Impressed, 19th c

G

1 Bow, London, England. Porcelain, 1744–60

2 Bow, London, England. Porcelain, 1750–70

3–4 Tavernes, France. Faïence, 1760–80

5 Faenza, Italy, 15th century. The town of Faenza gave its name to faïence

6 Buen Retiro, Madrid, Spain. Soft-paste porcelain, 1759–1808

7 Gotha, Germany. Hard-paste porcelain. Painted blue, 1775–1800

8 Gotha, Germany. Painted blue, 1805–30

9 Unger, Schneider, Thuringia, Germany, 1861–87

10 Nicolas Gardin, Rouen, France, c. 1760

11 Limoges, France, 1842–98

12 Swansea, Wales, 1765–1870

13 Emile Galle, Nancy, France, early 20th c

14 Guy Green, printer, Liverpool, England, 1756–99

15 Limoges, France, c. 1773

16 Alcora, Spain. Faïence/porcelain, c. 1750

H

1–2 Hannong, Faubourg St Lazare, Paris, France, c. 1773

3 Strasburg, Germany. Faïence/porcelain, c. 1750

4 Nevers, France. Faïence, 17th c

5 D Hofdick, 'De Ster' (The Star), Delft, Holland. Faïence, c. 1705

6 Antoine de la Hubaudière, Quimper, France, c. 1782

7 Faincerie de la Grande Maison, Quimper, France, c. 1898–1902

8 Delft, Holland. Faïence, 17th c

9–10 Hannon & Laborde, Vincennes, France, c. 1765

11 Prague, Germany. Porcelain, 1810–35

12 Humphrey Palmer (potter), Hanley, England, c. 1760

13 Winterthur, Switzerland. Faïence, 17th c

14 Leeds, England. Pottery, c. 1750

15 Hugo Booth, Stoke-on-Trent, England, c. 1785

16 Henry Roudeburth, Montgomery, Pennsylvania, USA, early 19th c

1 h 2 h 3 H

4 H. 5 H 6 HB

7 HB 8 HDK 9 H·L·

10 h l l 11 HK

12 H.P.

13 HP 1636

14 HARTLEY, GREEN & CO.

15 H. BOOTH

16 Henry Roudebuth April 28th 1811

I

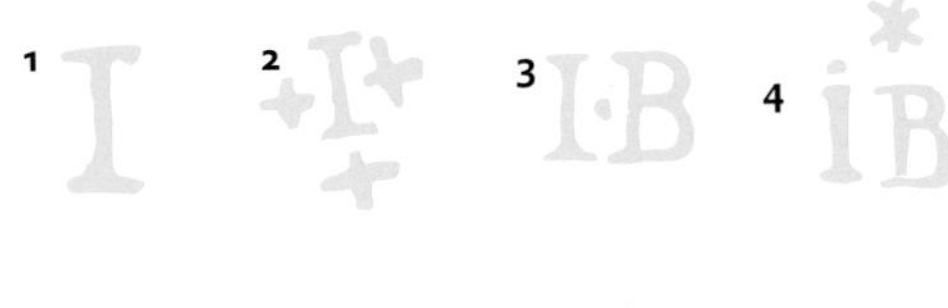

5 I.C.

6 I.E.1697

7 I.W

8 IE:W:1699: WROT:HAM

9 I.Smith

10 IRESON

11 I. & G. RIDGWAY

12 IRONSTONE B & M

13 I. SEYMOUR TROY

14 I. B. FARRAR & SONS

15 I. DALE BURSLEM

16 IAG 9

1 Bow, London, England. Painted red or blue, 1744–59

2 St Cloud, France. Faïence/porcelain, 1678–1766

3 Bristol, England. Painted blue or gold, 1770–81

4 'De Ster' (The Star), Delft, Holland. Faïence. Painted blue, c. 1764

5 John Crolius, New York, USA. Impressed, c. 1790

6–8 Variations on mark from Wrotham, England. Slipware, 17th or 18th c

9 Joseph Smith, Wrightstown, Pennsylvania, USA, c. 1775

10 Nathaniel Ireson (potter), Wincanton, England. Tin-glazed earthenware, 1740–50

11 Job Ridgway, Hanley, Staffordshire, England. Earthenware, 1802–08

12 Bagshaw & Meir, Burslem, Staffordshire, England. Earthenware. Printed or impressed, 1802–08

13 Israel Seymour, Troy, New York, USA. Impressed, c. 1825

14 Isaac Farrar, Fairfax, Vermont, USA, c. 1800

15 J Dale (potter), Burslem, Staffordshire, England, Late 18th c – early 19th c

16 Lisbon, Portugal, c. 1773

J

1 Longton Hall, Newcastle, England. Porcelain/ stoneware, 1750–60
2 Ilmenau, Thuringia, Germany. Faïence/ porcelain, c. 1777
3 Ilmenau, Thuringia, Germany, 1900–40
4 Copenhagen, Denmark, 1750–60
5 Aprey, France. Faïence, c. 1750
6 J Dimmock & Co, Hanley, Staffordshire, England, late 19th c
7 G Jones & Sons, Stoke-on-Trent, England, late 19th c – early 20th c
8 James Hadley & Sons, Worcester, England, 1896–1903
9 Bell Works, Shelton, England. Pottery. Printed, 1770–1854
10 St Cloud, France. Soft-paste porcelain, 1678–1766
11 Jacob Petit (potter), Fontainebleau, France. Hard-paste porcelain. Painted blue, c. 1800
12 Jean Pouyat (potter), Limoges, France. Painted red, 1842
13 John Remney, New York, USA. Stoneware, c. 1775
14 Joseph Robert (potter), Marseilles, France. Porcelain, 1754–93
15 Ashby Potters Guild, Burton-on-Trent, England. Pottery, early 20th c

K

1 Klosterle, Bohemia, Germany. Porcelain, lead-glazed earthenware, 1794–1803

2 Jan Kuylich, Delft, Holland. Faïence. Painted blue, 17th c

3 Jan Kuylich the younger, Delft, Holland. Faïence. Painted blue, registered 1680

4 Kiel, Germany. Faïence, c. 1770

5 Meissen, Germany. Hard-paste porcelain, 1720–60

6 Königliche Hof Conditorei, Meissen, Germany. Hard-paste porcelain. Painted blue, 1720–60

7 Königliche Porzellan Manufaktr, Meissen, Germany. Hard-paste porcelain. Underglaze blue, c. 1723

8 Krister, Germany, 19th c

9 Keeling (potter), Hanley, Staffordshire, England. Impressed, 1806–24

10 Keller & Guerin (owners), Lunéville, France. Faïence, 1778

11 Kiev, Russia. Porcelain, 1798–1850. Stoneware, 1800–11

12 Joseph Kishere (potter), Mortlake, England

13 Klum, Germany. Porcelain, 1800–50

14 Smith-Phillips China Co, East Liverpool, Ohio, USA, late 19th c

15 Knowles, Taylor & Knowles, East Liverpool, Ohio, USA. Established 1854

L

1–3 Jean-Joseph Lassia (proprietor), Paris, France, 1774–84

4 Lille, France. Hard-paste porcelain, late 18th c

5 Tours, France. Faïence, c. 1756

6 Valenciennes, Nord, France. Faïence, 1735–80

7 Limbach, Thuringia, Germany. Hard-paste porcelain. Painted red, c. 1772

8 Buen Retiro, Spain. Soft-paste porcelain, 1759–66

9 Valenciennes, Nord, France. Faïence, hard-paste porcelain, c. 1785

10 St Cloud, France. Faïence, porcelain, 1678–1766

11–13 Leeds, England, Creamware, late 18th c

14–16 Limbach, Thuringia, Germany, late 18th c

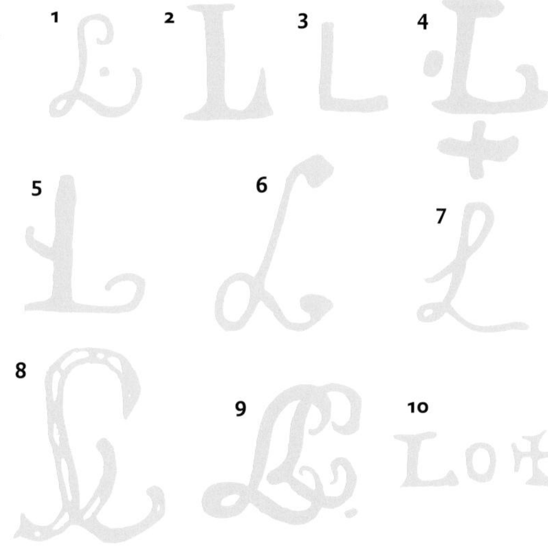

11 LEEDS POTTERY

12 LEEDS · POTTERY
LEEDS · POTTERY

13 LEEDS ✱ POTTERY

14 **15** **16**

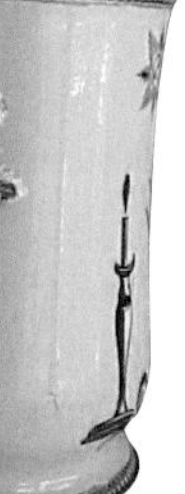

Leeds creamware mug, c. 1780s

M

1–2 Rouen, France, 1720–30

3–4 Minton, Stoke-on-Trent, England. Underglaze blue, 1800–30

5 Longton Hall, Newcastle, Staffordshire, England, 1750–60

6–7 Pierre Roussencq (founder), Marans, France. Faïence, late 18th c

8 Moreau Ainé, Limoges, France, late 19th c

9 Arnoldi, Germany, early 19th c

10 Mennecy, France. Porcelain, 1734–73

11 Herculaneum, Liverpool, England, 1833–41

12 Schmidt Brothers, Germany, late 18th c

13 Mason, Fenton, England. Faïence. Printed, 1813

14 Meissner Porzellan Manufaktur, Dresden, Germany. Hard-paste porcelain, c. 1723

15 Minton & Boyle, Stoke-on-Trent, England. Impressed, 1836–41

16 Mayer & Newbold (potters), Hanley, England, early 19th c

N

1 Niderviller, France. Faïence, mid- to late 18th c

2 Derby, England. Incised blue or red, c. 1770

3 New Hall, Shelton, England. Painted red, 1782–1810

4 New Hall, Shelton, England. Painted black, 1782–1810

5 Nove, Venice, Italy, 1800–25

6 Limbach, Germany. Porcelain, late 18th c

7 Wrotham, England, 17th c

8 Bristol, England. Pottery, porcelain. Overglaze blue or gold, 18th c

9 Urbino, Italy. Pottery, 16th c

10 Christian Nonne & Roesch (owners), Ilmenau, Thuringia, Germany. Porcelain, c. 1786

11 Nantgarw, Wales. Hard-paste porcelain. Painted red, c. 1811

12 Newcastle-upon-Tyne, England. Pottery. Impressed, c. 1800

13 New Hall, Shelton, England. Painted red, late 18th c

14 Nottingham, England. Pottery, c. 1705

15 Niderviller, France. Faïence, late 18th c

16 Bassano, Italy. Soft-paste porcelain, c. 1760

O

1 Bow, London, England. Porcelain, c. 1750

2 St Petersburg, Russia. Porcelain, c. 1760

3 Mennecy-Villeroy, France. Porcelain, faïence, mid-18th c

4 Mennecy-Villeroy, France. Porcelain, faïence. Painted blue, c. 1773

5 George Oswald (painter and potter), Ansbach, Bavaria, Germany, 1692–1733

6 Oscar Schlegelmilch, Thuringia, Germany, late 19th c

7 Ohio Valley China Co., Wheeling, West Virginia, USA, c. 1890

8 Olerys & Laugier (managers), Moustiers, France. Hard- and soft-paste porcelain, c. 1739

9 Ott & Brewer, Trenton, New Jersey, USA, c. 1880

10 Brampton, England. Brownware, c. 1825

11 Olivier (potter), Paris, France. Faïence, late 18th c

12 Cambrian, Wales. Earthenware, c. 1807

13 Baker, Bevans & Irwin, Swansea, Wales, c. 1830

14 J & G Alcock, Cobridge, England, mid- to late 19th c

15 Duke of Orleans (patron), Loiret, France, mid-18th c

16 J B Owens Pottery Co., Zanesville, Ohio, USA, c. 1890

P

1–2 Seth Pennington (potter), Liverpool, England. Painted gold or colour, late 18th c

3–4 James & John Pennington (potters and painters), Liverpool, England. Painted gold or colour, mid-18th c

5–6 Pinxton, Derbyshire, England. Soft-paste porcelain, 1796–1813

7 St Cloud, France. Faïence, porcelain, mid-18th c

8 Nymphenberg, Germany. Porcelain. Impressed or incised, mid-18th c

9 Philippe-Auguste Petit (potter), Lille, France. Painted colour, c. 1778

10 Pigory (owner), Chantilly, France. Soft-paste porcelain, early 19th c

11 Rouen, France. Faïence. Painted colour, 16th or 17th c

12 Moustiers, France. Faïence, mid-18th c

13 Paul Hannong (proprietor), Strasburg, France. Underglaze blue, 1740–60

14 Paris, France, 1786–1793

15 Plymouth Pottery Co., Plymouth, England, c. 1850

16 Moulins, France. Faïence, c. 1730.

R

1 Louis-François Roubiliac (sculptor), Chelsea, London. Impressed, c. 1738

2 Bristol, England. Porcelain, c. 1750

3 Marseilles, France. Porcelain, 1773–93

4 Bow, London, England. Porcelain, 1750–60

5 Joseph Gaspard Robert (potter), Marseilles, France. Faïence, 1754–93

6–7 Rauenstein, Thuringia, Germany. Porcelain, 1783

8 Rouen, France, 16th–17th c

9 Bow, London, England. Porcelain, 1750–60

10 Sèvres, France. Hard- and soft-paste porcelain. Painted blue, gold, 1793–1804

11 Meissen, Germany. Hard-paste porcelain. Underglaze blue, c. 1730

12 Rainforth (potter), Leeds, England, late 18th or early 19th c

13 Rockingham, Swinton, Yorkshire, England, late 18th or early 19th c

14 Worcester, England. Hard-paste porcelain, 1756–1774: 'Made by R Hancock'

15 William Reid (potter), Liverpool, England. Porcelain. Impressed, 1755–59

16 Ralph Toft (potter), Wrotham, England. Slipware, c. 1677

S

1 St Petersburg, Russia. Hard-paste porcelain. Painted blue, c. 1744

2–3 Caughley, England. Hard-paste porcelain. Painted blue, 1755–99

4 Rouen, France. Faïence, c. 1760

5 St Cloud, France. Faïence, porcelain, 1678–1766

6 Eisenach, Germany, mid- to late 19th c

7 Schlaggenwald, Bohemia, Germany. Porcelain, 1793–1866

8 Joseph Flower (painter), Bristol, England. Delft, 1739–51

9–10 Jacques Chapelle (potter), Penthiève factory, Sceaux, Seine, France. Soft-paste porcelain, 1749–63. Later 'Sceaux' painted in blue

11 Caughley, England. Porcelain, 1750–1814

12 Smith, Ambrose & Co., Burslem, Staffordshire, England, c. 1800

13 John Sadler (engraver), Liverpool, England. Pottery and hard-paste porcelain. Printed, 1756–70

14 Caughley, England. Porcelain. Impressed, 1750–1814

15 Spode. Stoke-on-Trent, England. Porcelain. Impressed. Painted red, blue, black or gold, c. 1770

16 Spode & Copeland, Stoke-on-Trent, England, 1770–97

T

1–3 Thomas Frye (manager), Bow, London. Porcelain, 1744–59

4 Tebo (modeller), Bristol, England. Porcelain, 1770–75

5 Tite Ristori, Nevers, France. Pottery, c. 1850

6 Torquay, Devon, England. Terracotta, 1875–1909

7 Nevers, France. Faïence, 18th c

8 T Vickers, Lionville, Pennsylvania, USA, c. 1805

9 Tannowa, Bohemia, Germany. Faïence, porcelain, 1813–80

10 Thomas Fell (potter), Newcastle, England, c. 1817

11 T Fletcher (owner), Shelton, England, 18th c

12 Thomas Toft (potter), Burslem, England. Slipware, c. 1670

13 Theodore Haviland, Limoges, France, c. 1920

14 Theodore Haviland, New York, USA. Printed green or black, c. 1936

15 Warne & Letts, South Amboy, New Jersey, USA, c. 1806

16 Theodore Deck, Paris, France. Faïence, c. 1859

U, V

1 J Uffrecht, Haldensleben, Germany, late 19th c
2 Sarreguemines, France. Faïence, porcelain, c. 1770
3 Nathaniel Hewelcke (potter), Venice, Italy. Porcelain. Incised, 1757–63
4 Villeroy & Boch, Mettlach, Saar, Germany, 1890–1910
5 Charles Vyse, Chelsea, London, early 20th c
6–7 Veuve Perrin (potter), Marseilles, France. Faïence. Painted black, c. 1790
8 Jan van der Kloot, Delft, Holland. Faïence. Painted blue, c. 1765
9 Baron Jean-Louis Beyerle, Niderviller, France. Faïence, 1754–70
10 Rue Thiroux factory, Paris, France. Hard-paste porcelain, c. 1775
11 Venice, Italy. Hard-paste porcelain, c. 1700
12 Villeroy & Bosch (potters), Mettlach, Germany. Faïence, c. 1842
13 Buen Retiro, Spain. Hard-paste porcelain, 1759–1808
14 Alcora, Spain. Porcelain, faïence, mid-18th c
15 Varages, France. Faïence, 18th c
16 Vinovo, Italy. Porcelain. Underglaze blue or incised, c. 1775

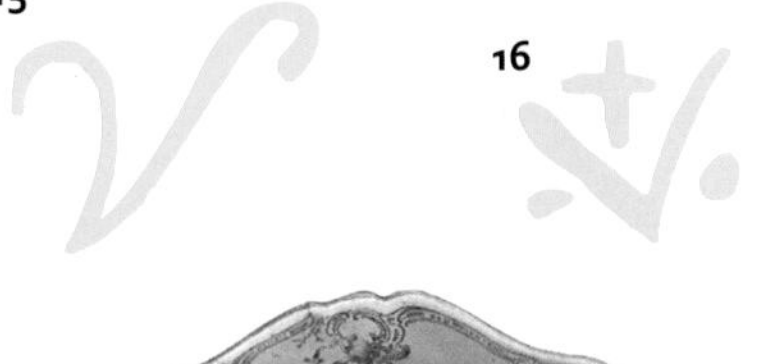

15

16

Veuve Perrin basin, c. 1760

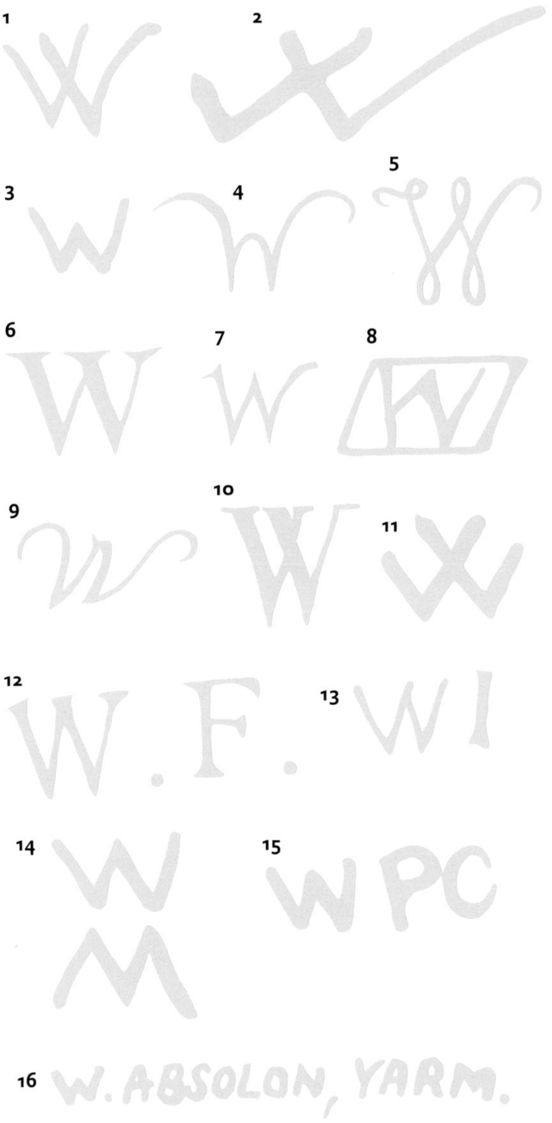

1 Plymouth, England. Hard-paste porcelain. Painted blue, c. 1768

2 Plymouth, England. Painted red, blue, gold, c. 1768

3 Thomas Wolfe (potter), Stoke-on-Trent, England. Impressed, 18th–19th c

4–8 Variations of the Worcester mark. Hard-paste porcelain, 1775–83

9 Rouen, France. Faïence, c. 1720

10–11 Wegeley (founder), Berlin, Germany. Porcelain, 1751–60

12 Bristol, England, c. 1853

13 Chelsea, London, England. Porcelain, 1745–84

14–15 Variations of the Worcester mark, late 18th c

16 Absolon (enameller), Yarmouth, England, c. 1800

W, X, Y, Z

1 John Walton (potter), Burslem, England. Earthenware, 18th–19th c
2 Wedgwood & Bentley, Staffordshire, England. Earthenware, 1769–80
3 Wedgwood, Etruria, England. Pottery. Impressed, c. 1771
4 Wedgwood, Etruria, England. Impressed on pottery, 1771. Printed red, blue, gold on porcelain, 1812–16
5–6 Ralph Wedgwood, Ferrybridge, England. Stoneware. Impressed, 1796–1800
7 Wedgwood. Pottery, After 1891
8 Wedgwood. Pottery. Impressed, after 1780
9 Wincanton, Bristol, England. Earthenware, 17th c
10–11 Vaux (or Bordeaux), France. Hard-paste porcelain, late 18th c
12 'De Griekse A' (The Greek A), Delft, Holland, c. 1674
13–15 Zurich, Switzerland. Pottery, hard-paste porcelain. Painted blue, late 18th c
16 Worcester, 1775–85

1 Walton
2 W. & B.
3 Wedgwood
4 WEDGWOOD
5 WEDGWOOD & CO
6 Wedgwood & Co. Ferrybridge
7 WEDGWOOD ENGLAND
8 WEDGWOOD
9 WINCANTON
10
11
12
13
14
15
16

Ceramic makers' marks: symbols

Anchors

1–4 Chelsea, London, England. Porcelain. Underglaze blue, gold, 1750–69

5 Chelsea, London, England. Soft-paste porcelain. Painted gold or red, c. 1745

6 Chelsea, London, England. Soft-paste porcelain. Underglaze blue or red, blue, purple, 1749–56

7 Derby-Chelsea, England. Porcelain. Painted blue, lilac or gold, c. 1770

8 Derby, England. Porcelain, c. 1745

9 Bow, London, England. Hard-paste porcelain. Painted red or blue, c. 1744

10 Bow, London, England. Soft-paste porcelain. Painted red or brown, c. 1760–80

11–12 Bow, London, England. Soft-paste porcelain. Painted red, brown or blue, c. 1760–80

13 Bow, London, England. Porcelain, 1745–70

14 Liverpool, England. Cream earthenware, 1793–1841

15 Sceaux factory, Seine, France. Porcelain, faïence, c. 1775

16 Thomas Fell (potter), Newcastle, England. Impressed, 18th–19th c

Animals, fishes and insects

1 Furstenberg, Germany. Porcelain, 18th c
2 Hesse Cassel, Germany. Hard-paste porcelain. Painted blue, c. 1763
3 Oiron, France, 16th c
4 'De Klauw' (The Claw), Delft, Holland, mid-18th c
5 Edgem Malkin, Burslem, England, late 19th c
6 Williamson, Longton, England, early 20th c
7 Frankenthal, Bavaria, Germany. Hard-paste porcelain. Painted blue, c. 1754
8 Amsterdam, Holland. Hard-paste porcelain. Painted blue, c. 1772
9 Rockingham, Swinton, England. Hard-paste porcelain. Painted red, c. 1824
10 Belleek, Ireland, c. 1860
11 Ralph Wedgwood, Burslem, England, 1796–1800
12 Lille, France. Hard-paste porcelain. Stencilled and painted red, c. 1784
13–14 Nyon, Switzerland. Hard-paste porcelain. Underglaze blue, c. 1780
15 Seville, Spain. Glazed pottery, 19th c

Arrows

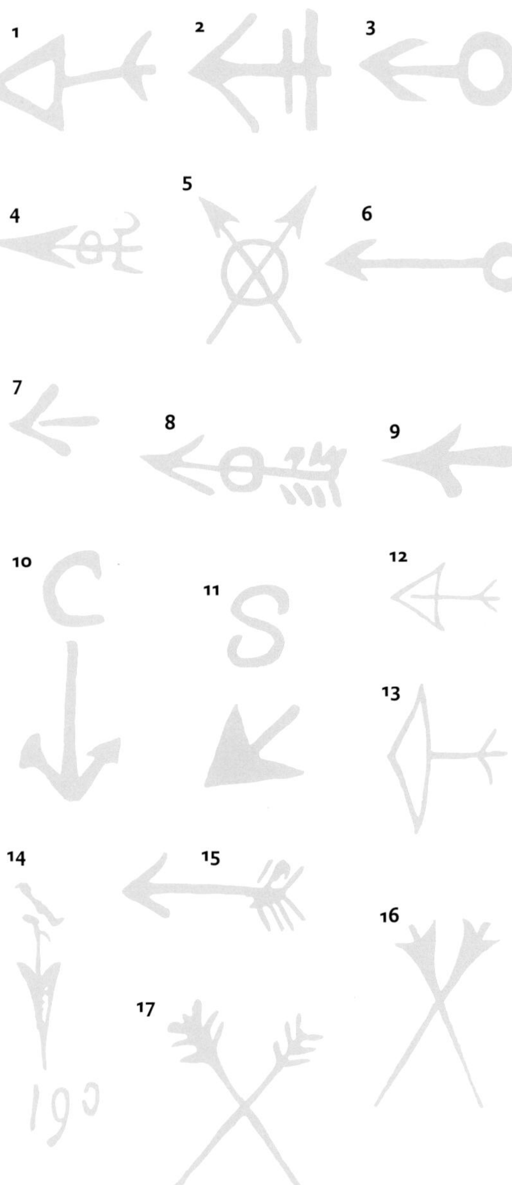

1–5 Bow, London, England. Porcelain, c. 1750

6 Plymouth, England. Hard-paste porcelain. Painted blue, 1768–70

7–8 Leeds, England. Pottery. Impressed, c. 1774

9–11 Caughley, England. Hard-paste porcelain. Painted blue, mid-late 18th c

12 Derby, England. Porcelain, c. 1830

13 Derby, England. Porcelain, 1745–1848

14 Robert Allen (painter), Lowestoft, England. Porcelain, 1757–80

15 W Absolon (enameller), Yarmouth, England. Porcelain, earthenware. Impressed, early 19th c

16 Rue de la Roquette factory, Paris, France. Hard-paste porcelain. Painted blue, c. 1774

17 La Courtille factory, Paris, France. Hard-paste factory. Underglaze blue, incised, c. 1771

Birds

1–2 Ansbach, Bavaria, Germany. Hard-paste porcelain. Painted blue, c. 1765

3 J V Kerckof (artist), Amsterdam, Holland, 1755–70

4–5 Herculaneum factory, Liverpool, England, c. 1833

6 Charles Ford, Burslem, England, 19th c

7 Boulton, Machin & Tennant, Tunstall, England, late 19th c

8 T Rathbone, Tunstall, England, early 20th c

9 Limoges, France, 1842–98

10 Sèvres, France. Hard-paste porcelain. Painted red, c. 1810

11 Sèvres, France. Hard-paste porcelain, c. 1852

12 Homer Laughlin China Co, East Liverpool, Ohio USA, late 18th c

13 W H Goss, Stoke-on-Trent, England, late 19th c

14 T Mayer, Stoke-on-Trent, England, c. 1829

15 Florence, Italy. Faïence, late 19th c

16 Hanks & Fish, Swan Hill Pottery, South Amboy, New Jersey, USA, c. 1849

Circles

1–2 Faenza, Italy. Faïence, 16th–17th c

3 Spode, Stoke-on-Trent, England. Impressed, late 18th c

4 Hochst, Germany. Hard-paste porcelain. Painted blue, red, gold, 1750–65

5–6 Worcester, England. Hard-paste porcelain. Underglaze blue, late 18th c

7 Bow, London, England. Soft-paste porcelain, late 18th c

8 Ken & Binns, Worcester, England. Porcelain, 1852–62

9 Wedgwood & Bentley, Etruria, England, 1769–80

10 Charles Field Haviland Co, Limoges, France, c. 1882

11 Enoch Wood & Sons, Burslem, England, c. 1790

12 Ilmenau, Germany. Porcelain, 19th c

13 Orléans, France. Hard-paste porcelain, c. 1800

14 Urbino, Italy. Pottery, 16th c

15 Cologne, Germany. Pottery, 17th c

16 Minton, Stoke-on-Trent, England. Hard-paste porcelain. Printed, 1800

Crescents

1–2 Bow, London, England. Porcelain, c. 1750–75
3–7 Caughley, England. Painted blue, c. 1775–99
8–11 Worcester, England. Hard-paste porcelain, c. 1751–1800
12 Nymphenburg, Germany. Porcelain. Impressed or incised, mid- to late 18th c
13 Pinxton, England. Soft-paste porcelain, 1796–1801
14 Turkey. Porcelain, c. 1850
15 Munden, Germany. Faïence, 18th c
16 Faenza, Italy. Faïence, 16th c

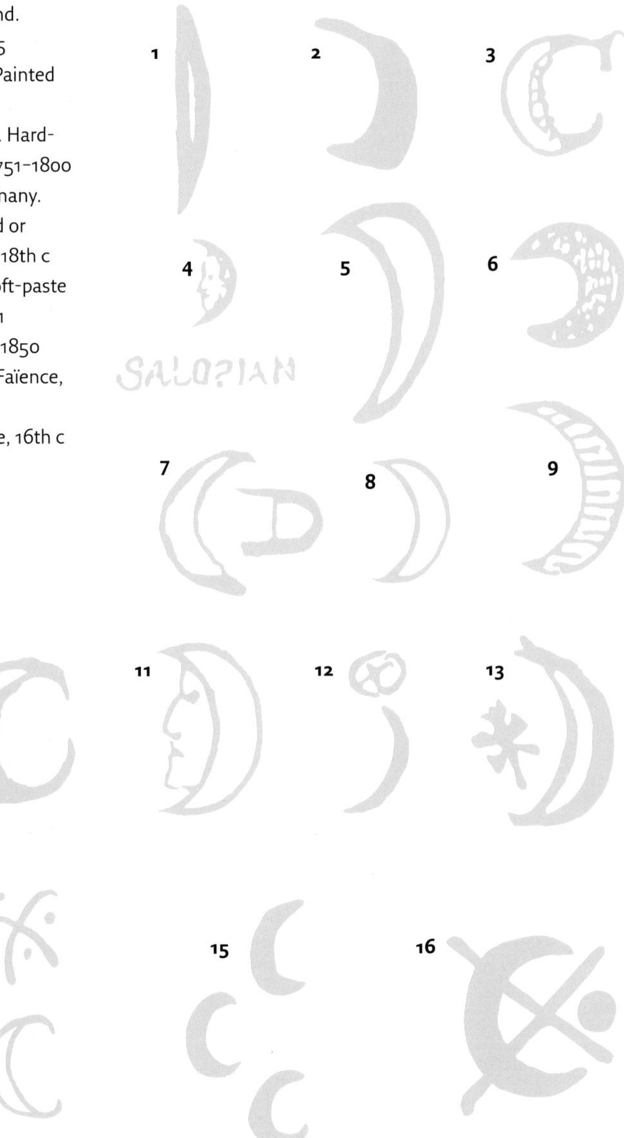

Lines and crosses

1 St Petersburg, Russia. Hard-paste porcelain. Painted blue, late 18th c

2 Royal Copenhagen Factory, Copenhagen, Denmark, 1830–45

3 Royal Copenhagen Factory, Copenhagen, Denmark, c. 1775

4 Varages, France. Faïence, c. 1770

5–6 Bristol, England. Porcelain. Painted colour, c. 1770

7 Leeds, England. Painted colour, c. 1770

8 Chelsea, London, England. Porcelain, 1745–84

9 Nymphenburg, Germany. Porcelain. Impressed or incised, late 18th c

10 Bow, London, England, mid-18th c

11 Copenhagen, Denmark, c. 1770

12–14 Bow, London, England, mid-18th c

15 Meissen, Germany, 19th c

16 Longton Hall, Staffordshire, England, 1749–60

17 Caughley, England, 1775–99

Teapot, Meissen, c. 1860

Crossed swords

1–8 Marks from the Meissen factory in Germany, all painted blue

1 Early 18th c

2–3 c. 1730

4–6 Mid-18th c

7–8 c. 1723

9 Worcester, England, mid-18th c

10 Bristol, England. Porcelain. Painted blue, gold, mid-18th c

11 Derby, England, mid-18th c

12 Coalport, Coalbrookdale, England, early 19th c

13 Samson, Edme, Paris, France, late 19th c

14 Caughley, England. Painted blue, 1775–99

15 Jacob Petit, Fontainebleau, France, 1830–40

16–17 Bristol, England. Porcelain. Painted blue or gold, 1773–81

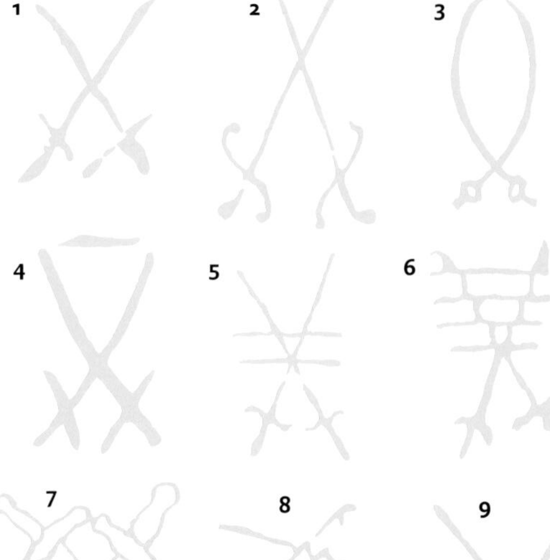

Crowns

1 Derby, England, 1775–70
2 Bloor, Derby, England, 1811–48
3 Vincennes, France. Hard-paste porcelain, c. 1765
4 Derby, England. Painted red or violet, c. 1780–84
5 Belleek, Ireland, Late 19th c
6 Worcester, England, c. 1813–40
7 Derby, England, c. 1784–1815
8 Royal Crown Derby, Derby, England, 1877–79
9 Sèvres, France, 1773
10 Sèvres, France, 1824–30
11 Meissen, Germany, 1720–50
12 Leeds, England. Earthenware, mid-18th c
13–14 St Petersburg, Russia. Porcelain. Painted colour, late 18th c
15 Herculaneum, Liverpool, England. Impressed or printed, 1800–41
16 James Clews (potter), Cobridge, England. Earthenware. Blue printed, c. 1819–29

Curves

1–5 Sèvres, France. Soft-paste porcelain, 1745–53
6–8 Sèvres, France. Soft- and hard-paste porcelain, 1764–71
9 Worcester, England, mid-18th c
10 Minton, Stoke-on-Trent, England, 1800–1831
11 Coalport, Coalbrookdale. Porcelain, early 19th c
12–13 Buen Retiro, Madrid, Spain, 1759–1808
14 Niderviller, France, late 18th c
15 Nuremburg, Germany, early 18th c
16 Nymphenburg, Germany, c. 1747

1 2 3 4 5 6 7 8 9

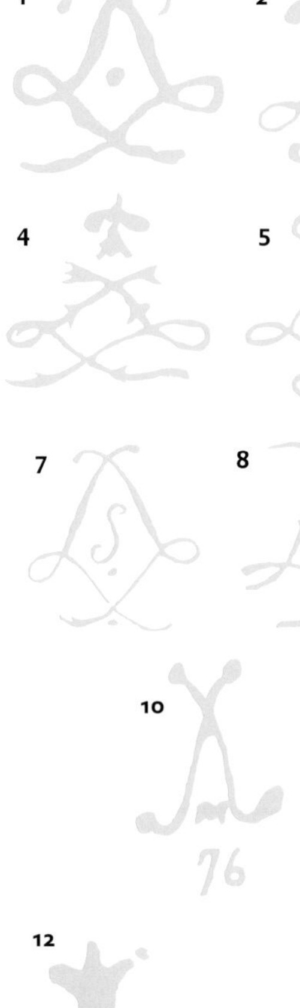

10 11

12 13

14 15 16

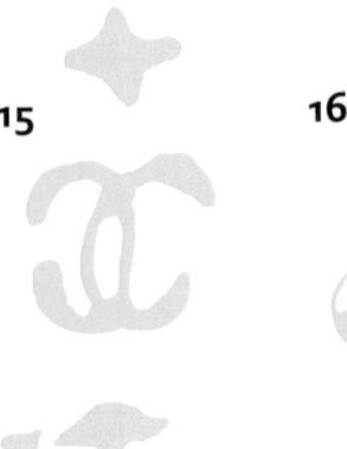

Nuremberg faience jug, early 18th century

Fleurs-de-lys

1 St Cloud, France. Soft-paste porcelain. Impressed, c. 1680–1766

2 Rouen, France. Faïence. Painted colour, 16th c

3 Bow, London, England. Soft-paste porcelain. Painted blue, c. 1730

4–5 Marseilles, France. Faïence, late 18th c

6–8 Buen Retiro, Madrid, Spain. Soft-paste porcelain, 1759–1808

9–10 Ginori, Italy. Painted blue, 1820–50

11 Minton, Stoke-on-Trent, England. Painted green, After 1850

12 Capo-di-Monte, Naples, Italy, 1730–40

13 Orléans, France, 1753–1812

14–15 Lowesby, England, mid-19th c

Flowers and trees

1–4 'De Roos' (The Rose), Delft, Holland, late 17th c

5 Longport, Staffordshire, England, c. 1825

6 Rose & Co, Caughley, England. Hard-paste porcelain. Painted colour, 1799

7 Coalport, Coalbrookdale, England, early 19th c

8 Volkstedt factory, Thuringia, Germany. Porcelain, late 18th c

9 Greuby Faïence Co, Boston, Mass., USA, c. 1900

10 Imenau, Germany. Faïence, porcelain, late 18th c

11 Limbach, Thuringia, Germany. Porcelain, late 18th c

12–13 Grosbreitenbach, Germany. Hard-paste porcelain. Painted colour, late 18th c

14 Berlin, Germany. Hard-paste porcelain. Painted blue, green or gold, c. 1800. Often on damaged pieces

15 Delft, Holland. Faïence, 18th c

16 'De Ster' (The Star), Delft, Holland. Faïence, c. 1720

Shields

1-2 Royal Factory, Vienna, Austria. Hard-paste porcelain. Painted blue, 1750-80

3-5 Royal Factory, Vienna, Austria. Incised, 1744-1820

6 Nymphenburg, Germany. Porcelain, 1754-1862

7-8 Nymphenburg, Germany, c. 1800

9 Ansbach, Germany. Hard-paste porcelain. Painted blue, mid- to late 18th c

10 Wood & Barker, Burslem, England, 19th c

11 Bridgwood & Son, Longton, England, 19th c

12 Enoch Wood & Sons, Burslem, England, 1818-46

13 Zell, Germany. Glazed earthenware, After 1818

14 Stoke-on-Trent, England. Porcelain, c. 1799

15 Copeland & Garrett, Spode, Stoke-on-Trent, England, 1833-47

16 Minton, Stoke-on-Trent, England, after 1868

Squares

1–4 Meissen, Germany. Bottger red stoneware, c. 1710–20
5 John & David Elers (potters), Newcastle, England. Stoneware, c. 1690–1710
6 Chelsea, London, England. Porcelain, 1745–85
7–11 Worcester, England. Porcelain, late 18th c
12 Derby, England. Painted blue, c. 1775
13–14 Bow, London, England, mid-18th c
15 Mayer & Newbold, Longton, Staffordshire, England. Painted red, 19th c
16 Baden, Germany, mid-18th c

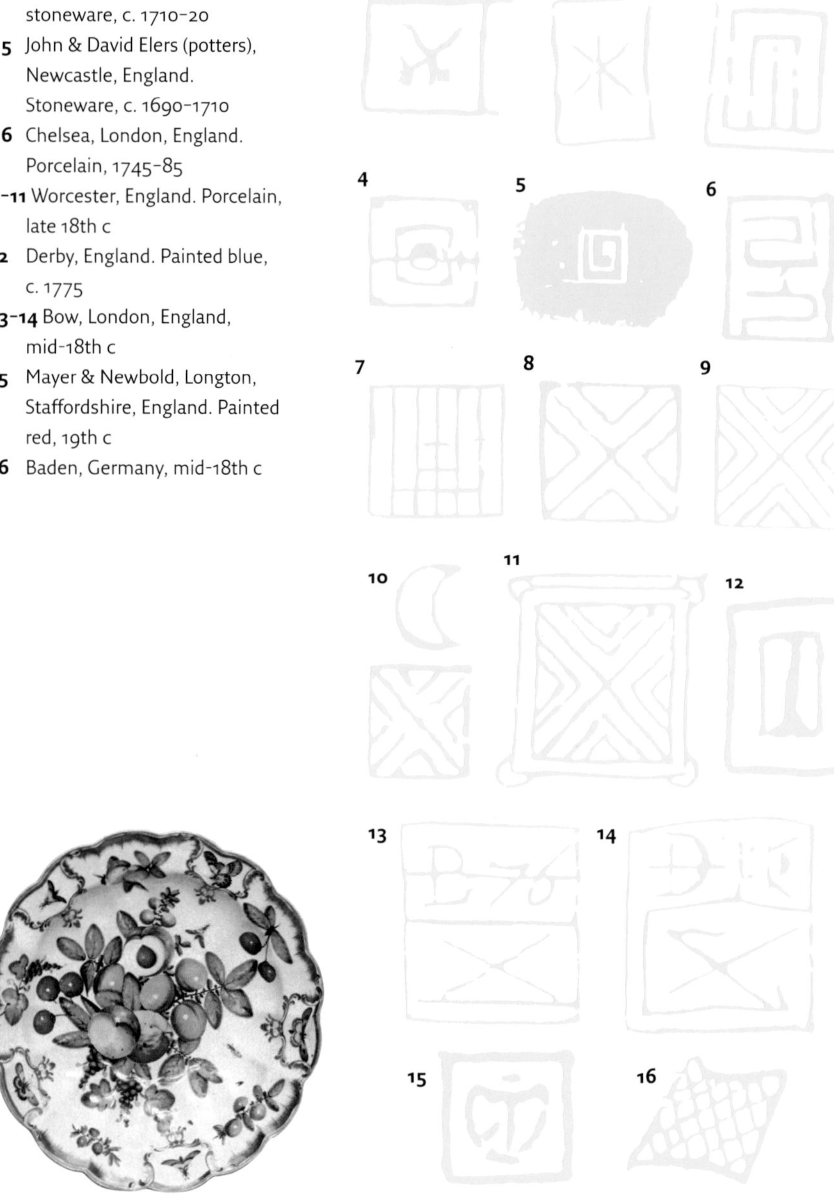

Chelsea dinner plate, c. 1750

Stars and suns

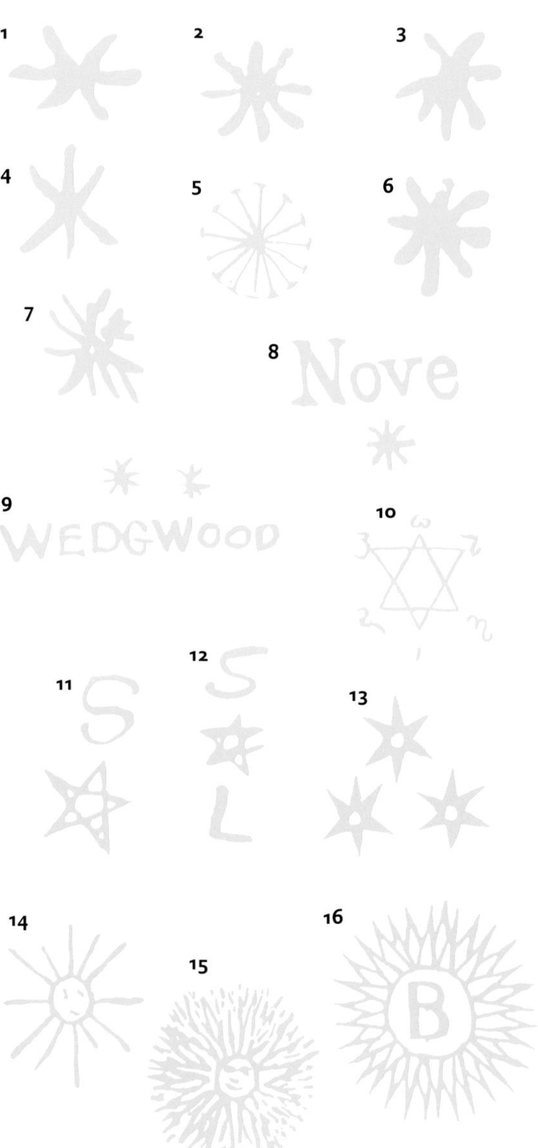

1 Isaac Farnsworth, Derby, England, 18th–19th c

2, 5, 6 Ginori, Doccia, Italy, 1735–07

3 Wallendorf, Thuringia, Germany. Porcelain, c. 1764

4 'De Ster' (The Star), Delft, Holland. Faïence, c. 1690

7 Caughley, England. Porcelain, c. 1750

8 Nove, Italy. Faïence, porcelain. Painted gold, mid-18th c

9 Wedgwood, Etruria, England. Impressed, 1765–1850

10 Nymphenburg, Germany. Hard-paste porcelain, late 18th c

11 Savona, Italy, 18th c

12 Seville, Spain, 19th c

13 Nevers, France. Faïence, 17th c

14–15 St Cloud, France. Soft-paste porcelain. Painted blue, 1678–1766

16 Robert Bloor, Derby, England, c. 1811–48

Triangles and hearts

1–2 Chelsea, London, England. Soft-paste porcelain. Painted gold or red, c. 1745–50

3–4 Bow, London, England. Incised. Painted blue, mid-18th c

5 Derby, England. Hard-paste porcelain. Impressed. Painted blue, mid-18th c

6 Bristol, England. Hard-paste porcelain. Impressed, c. 1763–73

7 Sèvres, France. 1900–02. Mark tells year of decoration

8 Meissen, Germany. Porcelain. Impressed, c. 1766–80

9 Burslem, England, 19th c

10 Sèvres, France. Hard-paste porcelain. Painted black. Soft-paste painted blue, c. 1900–11

11 Hanley, England, 19th c

12 Newcastle, England, 19th c

13 Orléans, France. Hard- and soft-paste porcelain. Painted colour, c. 1753–1812

14 Rue Popincourt factory, Paris, France. Porcelain, c. 1782–1835

15 Richard Chaffers, Liverpool, England, c. 1740–65

16 Bruges, Belgium, 18th c

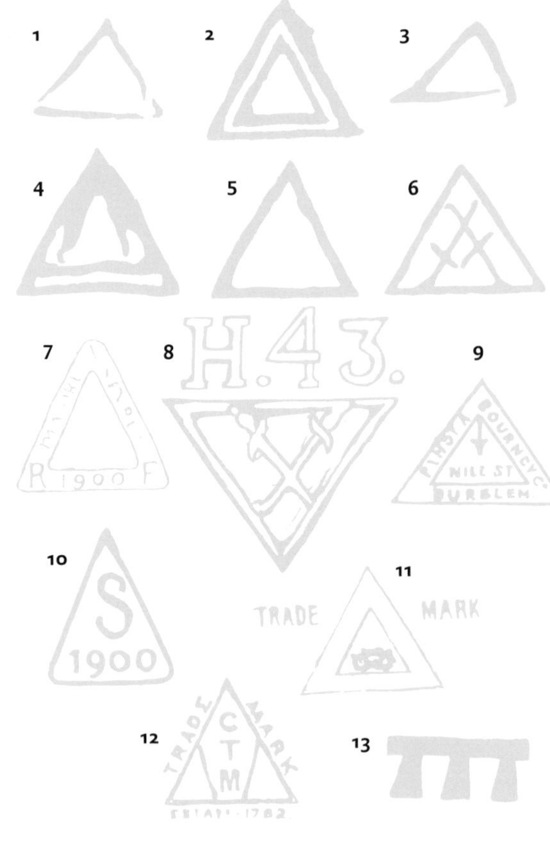

A Chelsea coloured acanthus leaf teapot and cover, c. 1750

Oriental copies

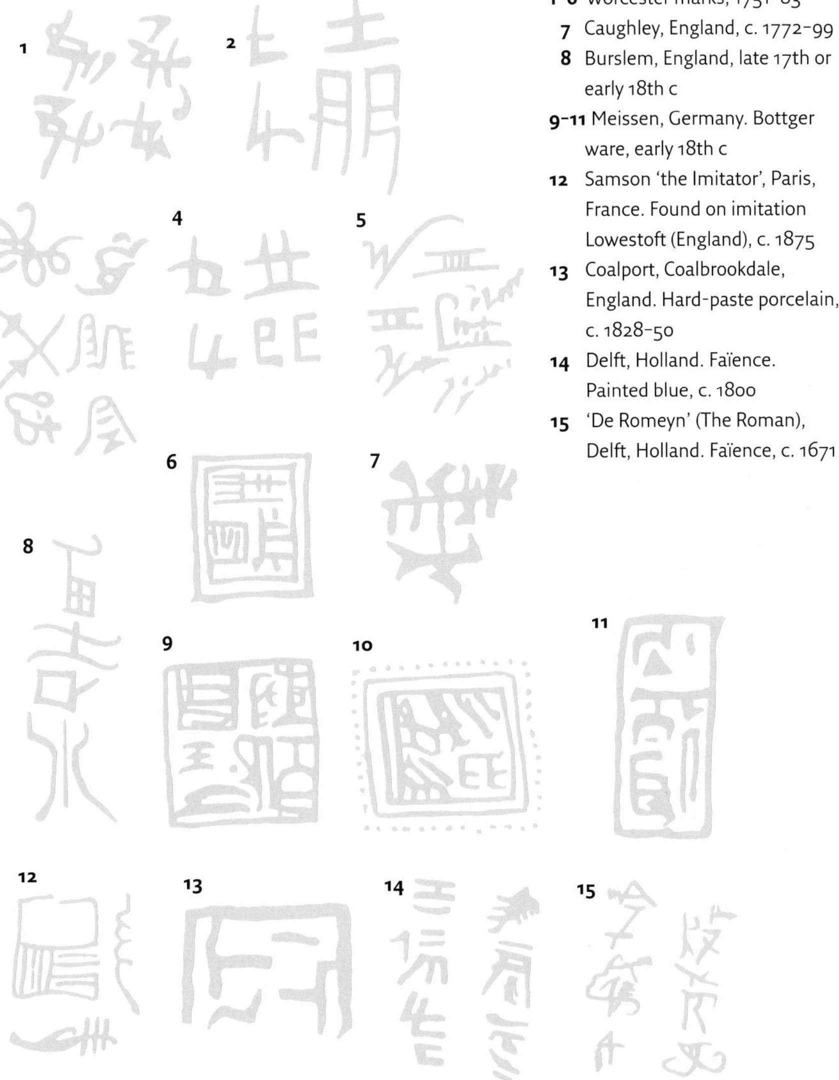

1–6 Worcester marks, 1751–83
7 Caughley, England, c. 1772–99
8 Burslem, England, late 17th or early 18th c
9–11 Meissen, Germany. Bottger ware, early 18th c
12 Samson 'the Imitator', Paris, France. Found on imitation Lowestoft (England), c. 1875
13 Coalport, Coalbrookdale, England. Hard-paste porcelain, c. 1828–50
14 Delft, Holland. Faïence. Painted blue, c. 1800
15 'De Romeyn' (The Roman), Delft, Holland. Faïence, c. 1671

Miscellaneous

1–2 T & R Boote, Burslem, England, late 19th c
3 Cobridge, Staffordshire, England. Painted blue, c. 1800
4 Delft, Holland. Faïence, 18th c
5 'De Oude Moriaan's Hooft' (The Old Moor's Head), Delft, Holland. Faïence, c. 1680
6 Royal Vienna Factory, Austria, c. 1850
7 Derby, England. Hard-paste porcelain. Painted blue, 1745–1848
8 Paris. Hard-paste porcelain. Painted gold, c. 1870
9 Caughley, England. Porcelain, 1750–1814
10 Clignancourt, France. Hard-paste porcelain, c. 1771–75
11 Worcester, England, c. 1751–83
12 Chantilly, France. Soft-paste porcelain. Painted blue or red, c. 1725–1800
13 J & M P Bell & Co., Scotland, late 19th c
14 Limoges, France. Hard-paste porcelain, c. 1736–96
15–16 Bellevue Pottery Co., Hull, England. Earthenware, c. 1825
17 Savona, Italy, 17th c
18 Cambrian factory, Swansea, Wales. Soft-paste porcelain, c. 1765
19 W T Copeland & Sons, Spode, Stoke-on-Trent, England. Porcelain, c. 1847
20 Burslem, England, c. 1795
21 Old Hall Pottery, England. Earthenware, 19th c
22 Tournay, Belgium. Soft-paste porcelain, late 18th c

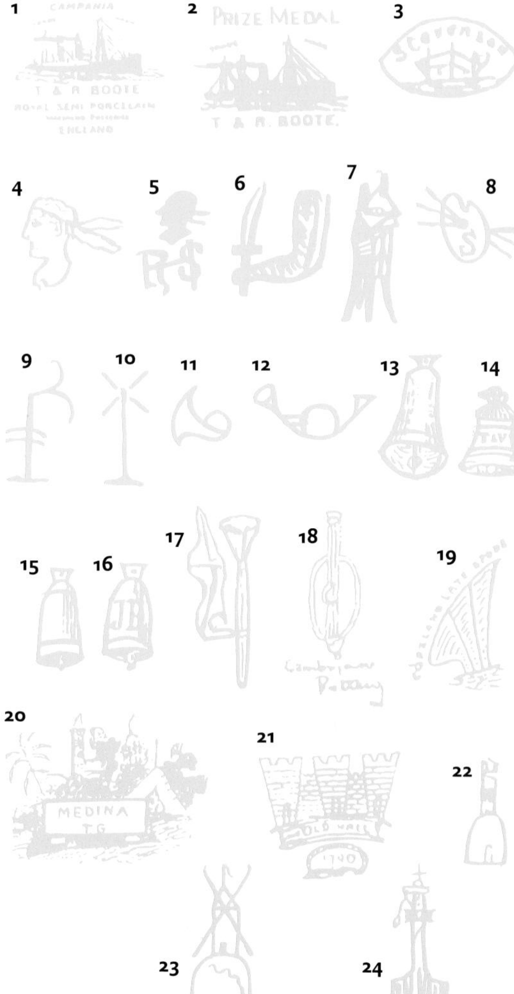

23 Clignancourt, France. Hard-paste. Painted blue, gold, c. 1771–98
24 Savona, Italy, 18th c

Miscellaneous

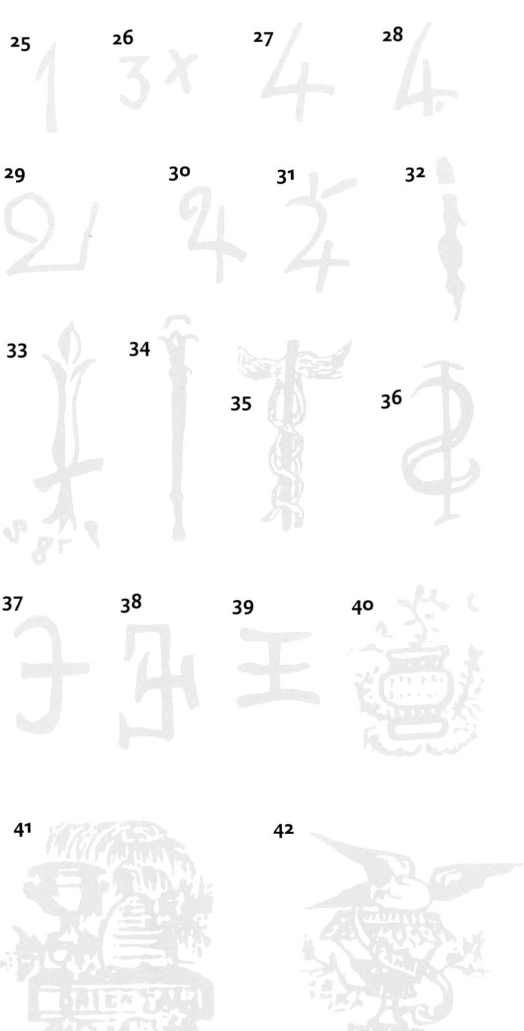

25–27 Bristol, England. Pottery, porcelain. Painted blue or gold, 18th c

28 Nevers, France. Pottery. Painted colour, 16th c

29–31 Plymouth, England. Hard-paste porcelain. Painted red, blue or gold, c. 1768

32–34 Royal Factory, Berlin, Germany. Hard-paste porcelain. Painted blue, c. 1760

35 Hanley, England, 19th c

36 Nymphenburg, Germany. Porcelain. Impressed or incised, late 18th c

37 Caughley, England. Hard-paste porcelain. Painted blue, c. 1750

38 Bow, London, England. Porcelain, c. 1750

39 Bristol, England. Hard-paste porcelain. Painted colour, c. 1770

40 Bristol, England. Hard-paste porcelain. Printed blue, c. 1800

41 Job Ridgways (potter), Shelton, England, c. 1794

42 Podmore, Walker & Co., Staffordshire, England, c. 1755

Leading pottery and porcelain manufacturers

must know

Factory marks are usually found on the base of an object. Variations in the mark can provide a basis for dating.

The factory marks may be in the form of the maker's initials, his full name, a symbol or coat of arms, or a combination of these.

Relatively few examples of English pottery or porcelain made before the 19th century bear a mark to indicate factory of origin.

Continental potters applied marks to some of their products as early as the 17th century.

A British mark including the work 'Limited' or 'Ltd' will not be earlier than 1860. 'Made in England' indicates 20th-century manufacture.

Belleek Established in Fermanagh, Ireland in 1857 by McBirney and Armstrong, the Belleek factory specializes in a lustrous mother-of-pearl effect on elaborate Parian openwork baskets and dishes with marine motifs.

Bennington John and William Norton established the Bennington Pottery in Vermont in 1793, eventually producing decorative salt-glaze wares, blue-and-white jugs and Parian ware. Between 1846 and 1858, the firm produced Bennington – or Rockingham – ware with a rich brown glaze often mottled with yellow, blue and orange.

Bonnin and Morris Founded in Philadelphia in the 1770s by Gousse Bonnin and George Anthony Morris, probably the first American factory to make soft-paste porcelain. Their ware is sometimes marked S for Southwark, or more frequently P for Philadelphia.

Bow Established by Thomas Frye and others in 1745, they produced blue-and-white soft-paste porcelain, the first in England on a commercial scale. Founded in Bow, Middlesex, moving to Stratford-le-Bow in 1749. Its vast output varied in appearance and quality, making identification difficult. It closed in 1775.

Bristol Earthenware was probably produced in Bristol in the late 13th century, but pottery-making was not fully established there until 1671. Edward Ward produced the first tin-enamelled earthenware at the Temple Black Pottery in 1683; soft-paste porcelain was produced from 1748 until 1752. Richard Champion made hard-paste porcelain in the city from 1773 to 1782, producing tea and coffee sets in the Sèvres style.

Caughley Established in 1775 as the Salopian China Manufactory by Thomas Turner. Best known for its soapstone porcelain, transfer-printed in black, sepia and blue, it also produced blue-and-white ware with a purple tinge to the blue, as well as plain blue gilded tableware. Acquired by John Rose of Coalport in 1799 and traded as Coalport/Caughley until transferred to Coalport in 1814.

Chelsea The Chelsea Porcelain Manufactory produced soft-paste porcelain between 1745 and 1784 in the Meissen and Sèvres styles. Five main periods, each one using different pastes and marks: the Incised Triangle period (1745–49) used a satin-like, creamy paste flawed with microscopic specks and a thickly applied glaze that ages with a yellowish tinge; the Raised Anchor period (1749–53) used a paste with a faintly greyish tone and thick, creamy glaze; the Red Anchor period (1753–56) is marked by the use of a thinner paste with a smooth, slightly blue even glaze; and, after a two-year closure of the factory, the Gold Anchor period (1758–69), which used harder, chalky white, more translucent glaze and a glassy glaze with a greenish tinge in places. In 1770, William Duesbury of Derby acquired the factory.

Coalport John Rose established the Coalport factory at Colebrookdale, Shropshire in 1795 and took over the Caughley works in 1799. From 1814 he produced a wide variety of willow pattern and transfer-printed ware, later producing finely translucent porcelain tableware with a characteristic rich-maroon ground colour and ornate decoration. In 1926 the firm moved to Stoke.

Copeland See **Spode**

Crown Staffordshire Established in Fenton, Staffordshire in 1830 by Henry Green, production continued after his death in 1859 as M Green & Co; the current title dates from about 1890. They specialized in toy tea and dinner services and miniature ornaments, making full-sized services in bone china with high-quality decoration from 1876. The firm also produced many reproductions of 18th-century porcelain.

Derby One of the major British potteries, the Derby Porcelain Manufactory first produced porcelain figures in 1749. Some of these Meissen-style figures were decorated in London by William Duesbury, who took over the renamed Derby Porcelain Company in 1755

must know

A British mark including the words 'Trade Mark' will not be earlier than 1862, when the Trade Mark Act was passed.

A mark giving the country of origin – without 'Made in' – usually indicates a piece dating after 1891.

Derby porcelain figurine

must know

Some English 18th-century wares bear a small mark, usually in the form of a numeral or symbol, to indicate to the factory foreman which decorator completed the design. A gilder's mark may appear on some pieces.

Doulton ware includes the incised initials of the potter and the two artists responsible for the incised and the painted decoration.

Bone china became the standard English porcelain body by 1815.

and produced a variety of tableware. Quality improved after the Chelsea factory was taken over in 1770. From 1786 to 1811, as Crown Derby, the factory produced bone china tableware with Japanese decoration. Known as Bloor Derby from 1811 to 1848 when quality dipped. The Old Crown Derby China Works (1848–1935) was set up using old Derby moulds. The Crown Derby Porcelain Company opened 1876; it acquired the royal imprimatur in 1890.

Doulton & Co In 1815 John Doulton became a partner in a small pottery in Lambeth, London, launching his own factory in 1826. Initially making industrial ware, the firm produced ornamental pottery after 1851, and mugs and jugs modelled on famous people. In 1872 the firm started the hugely popular Lambeth faïence. The firm became Royal Doulton in 1902; and Doulton & Co. of Burslem, Staffordshire, in 1882.

Fulham Established by John Dwight in 1671 to make salt-glazed wares, it later made tankards and jugs decorated with hunting scenes and famous notables. The decoration changed to a Japanese style in the 1860s.

Goss WH Goss set up the Falcon Pottery of Stoke in 1858 to specialize in paper-thin Parian hollowware, brooches, necklaces and other porcelain jewellery. The pottery is most famous for its fairings, miniature figures and groups for fairs and the holiday souvenir trade.

Leeds Pottery This Yorkshire pottery, operating from 1760 to 1878, was the main pottery to produce cream-coloured earthenware, made from a yellowish fine light clay with a rich glassy glaze. It used three main styles of decoration – Chinese, rococo and classic – often with hand-pierced designs.

Limoges A hard-paste porcelain factory was set up here in 1771. In 1784 it unsuccessfully planned to provide plain white ware for decoration at Sèvres; the factory thrived nevertheless, with its own range of decorated ware. The town is the main centre for French porcelain.

Liverpool Earthenware jugs and mugs were produced here in vast quantities during the 1660s, but it was not until the production of tin-enamelled earthenware after

1710 that the city's potteries made their name. Cream-coloured earthenware often decorated in blue was produced from the 1780s as well as soft-paste porcelain. Richard Chaffers, produced soapstone porcelain with high-quality enamelled decoration from 1756.

Mason's In 1813 Charles James Mason was granted a patent for the manufacture of 'English porcelain', developing a 'patent ironstone china'. The mass-produced, pseudo-oriental designs were highly coloured using machine-ground metallic oxides thickly applied over transfer-printed outlines. The factory was also famous for its octagonal jugs with reptilian handles.

Meissen The first and for a long time the best porcelain factory in Europe was established at Meissen in Saxony in 1710. The factory produced its first hard-paste porcelain in 1713, decorating the wares with landscapes, chinoiseries and flora. Its exquisitely decorated porcelain was in demand in Europe throughout the 18th century.

Minton In 1793 Thomas Minton set up his pottery in Stoke-on-Trent, Staffordshire, to produce first cream-coloured earthenware and pearl ware and, after 1796, bone china decorated with blue transfers in imitation of painted Nankin porcelain. The firm later produced tableware and cabinet ware of increasingly exotic design, with much gilding for foliage, vines and tendrils.

Nantgarw-Swansea After attempting in 1813 to produce soft-paste porcelain to rival Sèvres, William Billingsley of Nantgarw in South Wales moved to the Cambrian Pottery in Swansea, producing a distinctive, fine duck-egg porcelain. Returning to Nantgarw, he continued to work until 1822. His work is known for its high-quality painting, particularly of flowers.

Remney, John A German immigrant, John Remney established a pottery in New York during the mid-18th century to produce some of the first US stoneware. He continued to produce stoneware until 1820.

Rockingham Established in 1745 by Edward Butler at Swinton, Yorkshire, the factory first produced brown domestic earthenware. After 1786 it traded under a number of different names, producing creamware and

must know

Pattern names used to identify patterns are often found from the mid-19th century onwards.

Painted pattern names identifying flowers or views usually indicate good-quality, collectable, 19th-century porcelain.

Diamond-shaped registration marks indicate the piece was made in Britain between 1842 and 1883.

Rockingham service plate

Sèvres vase

stoneware, until John and William Bramfeld started to produce fine-quality bone china under the Rockingham name in 1826. Because of its bone ash content, Rockingham porcelain was intensely white and translucent and was highly decorated with gilding and rich enamels. The factory flourished, producing dinner and tea services, vases and statuettes for nobility, until 1837. It then went into rapid decline, closing in 1842.

Rookwood Inspired by the faïence from the Haviland potteries of Limoges in 1876, Louise McLaughlin formed the Pottery Club with 12 other women. This eventually became the Rookwood pottery of Cincinnati, Ohio, which until it closed in 1941, produced a wide range of vases and ornaments with a marked Japanese influence. The decoration, made by applying modelled flowers in asymmetrical designs onto coloured clay, was originally done by Shirayamadani, a Japanese potter. Many of the potters who worked at Rookwood subsequently established their own potteries, spreading its influence across the United States.

Sèvres (Vincennes-Sèvres) Originally established in Vincennes near Paris in 1738 and granted a 20-year monopoly in 1745 for the production of soft-paste 'porcelain in the style of the Saxon [Meissen] . . . painted and gilded with human figures'. At first quality was uneven, but J-J Bachelier's arrival as art director in 1751 and a royal imprimatur in 1753 transformed its output. In 1756 the factory moved to Sèvres, adopting a rococo style. It became noted for its exceptionally fine painting and its beautifully modelled biscuit porcelain figures. Sèvres adopted a new hard-paste porcelain and a range of pigments, allowing its artists to decorate its wares with colours as rich and detailed as oil paintings. Further developments in style and design during the 19th and 20th centuries have secured Sèvres's position as the leading porcelain manufacturer in France.

Spode service plate

Spode In 1762 Josiah Spode became general manager of Turner & Banks of Stoke-on-Trent, acquiring the factory in 1770. The firm produced cream-coloured earthenware, but Spode introduced the successful all-over transfer printing under the glaze in Staffordshire blue. From the mid-1790s Spode printed his own luminous blue on white pearl ware. In 1833 WT Copeland and Thomas Garrett took over the firm.

Sunderland The various potteries in Sunderland have produced a range of inexpensive domestic earthenware since 1740 and cream-coloured earthenware since about 1780, often decorated with purple or pink lustre.

Tucker, William Ellis In 1826 William Tucker began to produce the first true porcelain in the USA. John Hulme joined him in 1828 and a new factory was built in 1831 when Alexander Hemphill succeeded Hulme. Tucker died in 1832, but production continued until 1838.

Union Porcelain Works Established at Greenport, Long Island about 1857 by William Boch, making porcelain hardware. Taken over in 1888, it made hard-paste decorative porcelain ware. Other Greenport potters include Charles Cartlidge, who made porcelain from 1849 to 1856; William Bloor, who produced Parian ware from 1858 to 1862; and Edward Lycett, whose Faience Company produced porcelain as well as faïence.

Wedgwood Wedgwood was founded by Josiah Wedgwood at Burslem near Stoke-on-Trent in 1759. At first it specialized in green-glaze ware, and cream-coloured earthenware, named Queensware from 1765 after a commission from Queen Charlotte. In 1774 Wedgwood began making his famous blue Jasper stoneware still produced today; Wedgwood has made little porcelain, producing bone china only from 1812 to 1822 and again after 1878.

Worcester The Worcester Tonquin Manufactory was founded in 1751 and was bought up by Thomas Flight, jeweller to the royal family, in 1783. Flight added Royal to the title in 1788 to become the Royal Worcester Porcelain Company, a name it reverted to in 1862. At first the firm specialized in blue-and-white soapstone but after 1763 it produced high-quality porcelain with an oriental design, often on a blue ground. In 1798 it introduced bone china ware with enamel and gilded decoration, which is still in production today.

Wedgewood vase

Worcester vase

Methods of construction

Coiled pottery

Coiled work is perhaps the simplest way of forming pots, although very attractive and decorative results can be achieved with variations of the basic method.

a Accurate cylinders of clay are cut from a block with a coiler, rolled by hand or extruded.

b A base is formed by coiling one of the lengths around itself on a flat surface. The clay is pressed together in each part of the spiral to ensure that the base is firm and solid.

c Other cylinders of clay are coiled on top of one another around the edge of the base. As the end of one length is reached, another length is moulded onto it and the coiling continues.

d The pot is built into the desired shape, and the end of the final coil is smoothed into a rim. The ribbed sides of the pot can be smoothed out, or left in their attractive pattern.

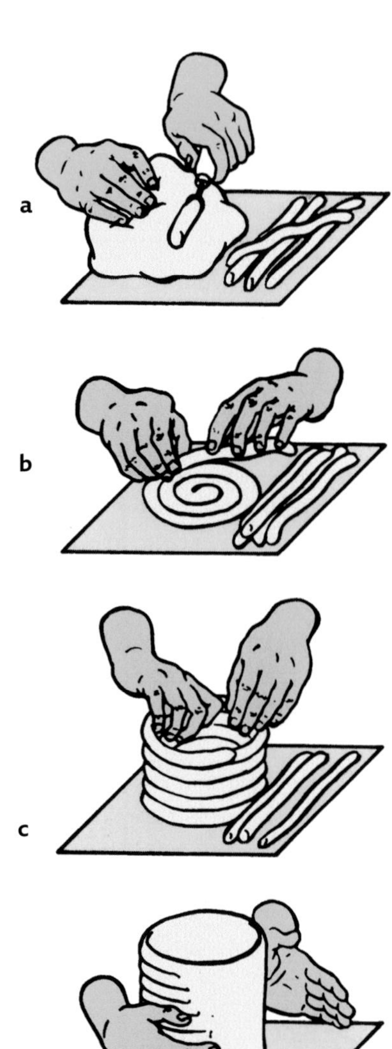

Thrown pottery

The basic principles of pot throwing apply to all kinds of pieces produced on the wheel, although of course the final size and shape of the pottery will depend on the potter's choice.

1 The clay is formed into a ball and held above the wheel, and then thrown onto the wheel as near the centre as possible. The wheel is then turned while the clay is manipulated into the exact centre and formed into a cone.

2 The potter uses his hands and various tools to press against the sides of the pot. He can increase the height of the pot, and shape the sides to the required contour.

4 The inside of the pot is smoothed in the same way as the outside – by the pressure and movement of the potter's hands and tools.

5 When the pot is the right shape and size, the potter cuts it free by drawing a wire between the pot and the wheel. The pot is then removed and allowed to dry before it is fired.

Moulded pottery

In press moulding, slabs of clay are pressed against a pre-formed shape (or mould), usually of plaster or clay. There are two types of press mould.

1 Clay is pressed over a hump mould to form a hollow vessel.

2 Clay is pressed into a hollow mould and the inside of the vessel is flattened with a sponge or with a rubber kidney.

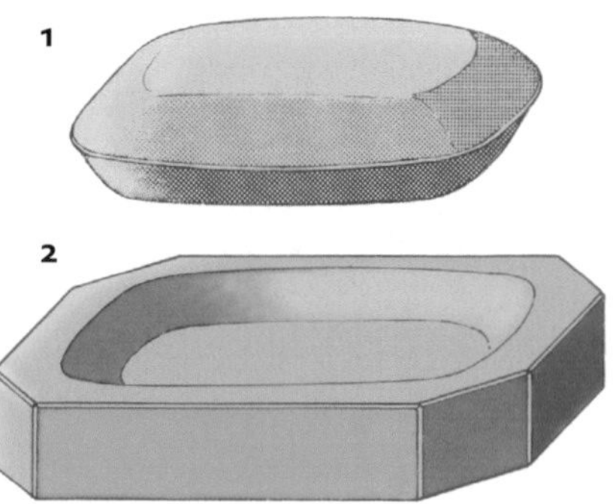

A plaster mould can be made in the following way:

a The shape is surrounded by a watertight barrier.

b Liquid plaster is poured around the shape.

c When the plaster has set, the completed mould is removed and dried.

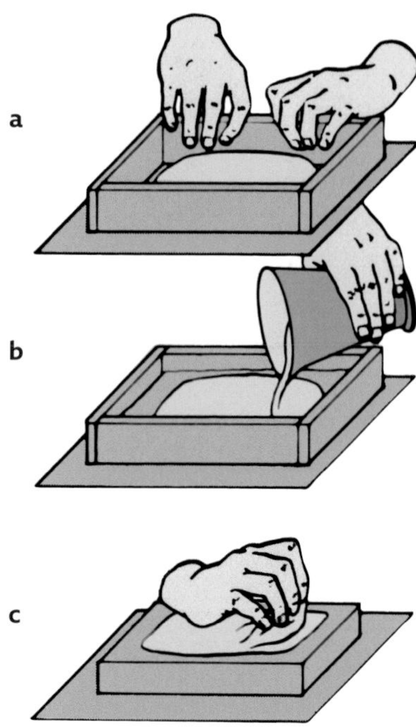

Raku pottery

The elementary steps towards producing raku pottery are described here, and pictured in the diagrams (left).

a The pottery is formed into the chosen shapes and given a preliminary firing; it is then covered with glaze.

b By means of the long-handled raku tongs, the pots are placed into a pre-heated kiln and become shiny; the pottery is then removed from the kiln.

c The hot pots are shut into an airtight container of combustible materials in order to produce the characteristic raku finish.

d Using the tongs, the pots are then plunged into hot water so that they cool very quickly.

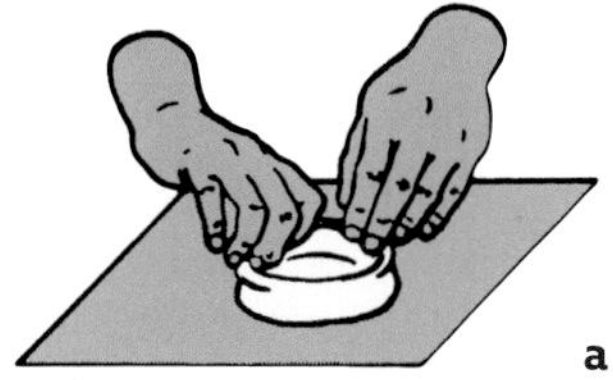
a

b

c

d

Raku bowl

Surface work

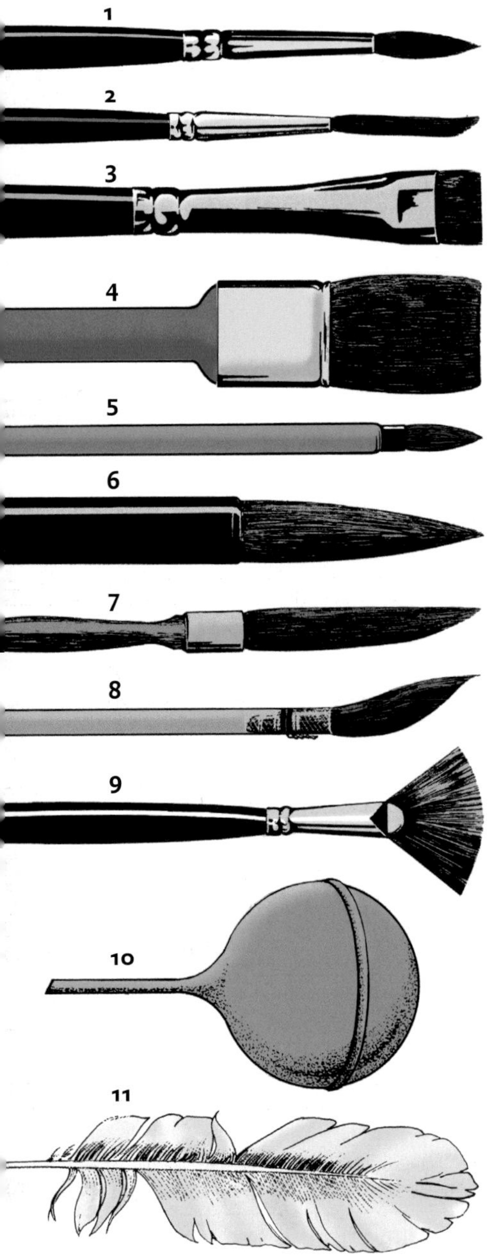

Applying colour

Various brushes and other pieces of equipment may be used to apply colour to the pottery. Some of these brushes are shown on the left, and the pot below illustrates the characteristic mark made by each tool.

1 **Round sable brush**
2 **Script brush**
3 **Short one-stroke brush**
4 **Flat duster**
5, 6 **Japanese brushes**
7 **Sword liner**
8 **Cut liner**
9 **Fan brush**
10 **Slip trailer**: a rubber bottle with a narrow spout, used for trailing lines of slip or glaze in patterns.
11 **Feather** used to draw one glaze into another in a decorative pattern.

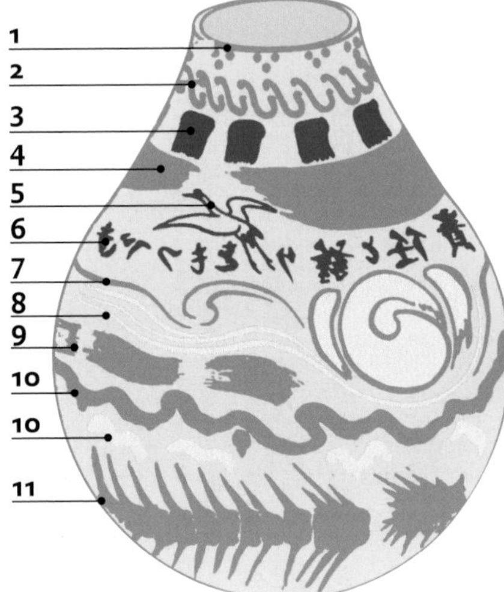

Relief tools

Some of the tools used to produce relief decoration on pottery are shown on the right. The lines of pattern on the pot below illustrate the characteristic marks made by each of the tools.

1 **Piercer**

2 **Clay plane**

3 **Bamboo tool**

4 **Tool handle**

5 **Ruler** used for making straight marks on the clay.

6 **Needle tool** used to produce stippled designs and to make fine lines.

7 **Quill** for producing a scratchy line.

8 **Loop tool**

9 **Sgraffito loop**

10 **Sgraffito tool**

11 **Texture brush** with stainless steel bristles.

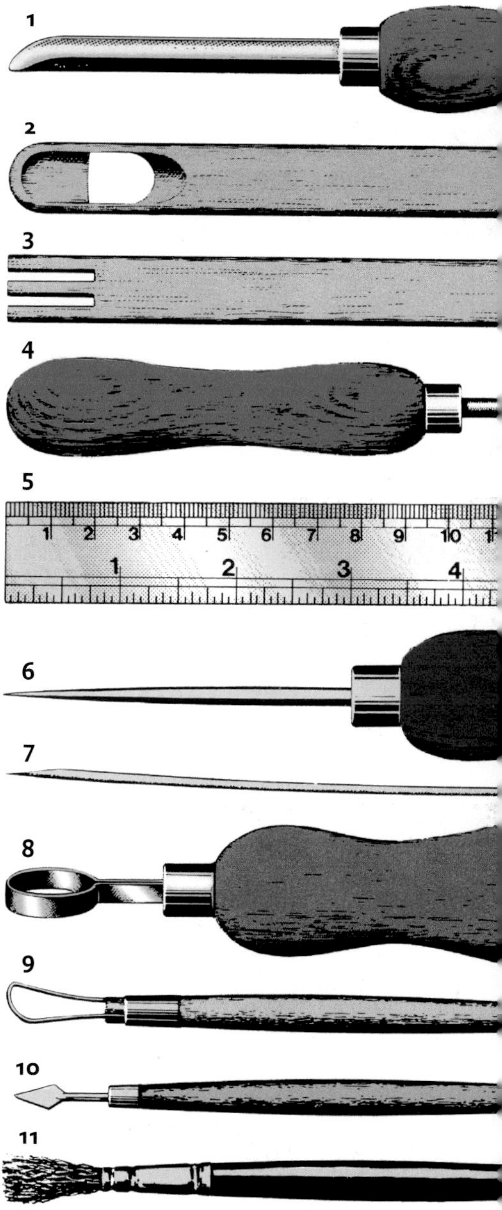

Oriental porcelain

The marks that appear on Chinese and Japanese wares are quite different from their Western counterparts – and not merely in the matter of script. Chinese marks do not refer to potters at all, but either indicate the emperor in whose reign a piece was made, or represent symbols of good omen or commendation.

False marks

Identifying oriental porcelain by its marks alone is difficult and potentially risky. The accurate identification of oriental ware requires above all a knowledge of period and factory styles: the marks can be regarded, at best, as a back-up.

Example of a six-character mark

Ming dynasty
Lung Ch'ing (Longqing), 1567–72

CHINESE PORCELAIN

Porcelain was a Chinese discovery in the 9th century CE. The great periods for Chinese porcelain are the reigns of the Ming and the Ch'ing emperors.

Reading Chinese marks

Chinese script reads in columns from right to left. To read them, go from top to bottom of the right-hand column, then top to bottom of the left. The first two characters signify the word 'great' (ta) (**1**), followed by the name of the dynasty (**2**). The next two characters represent the reign-name (**3**, **4**). The final two are 'period' (nien) (**5**) and 'make' (chih) (**6**). (There was also a dating system based on a 60-year cycle, rarely applied and difficult to interpret.)
In marks where there are only four characters, the dynasty is omitted. There is also an alternative form

consisting of a square seal mark, written in an archaic script known as 'seal character'.

Principal Chinese Dynasties

The Ming and Ch'ing (Qing) dynasties are the most important as regards Chinese porcelain. The Ming dynasty was established in 1368 and consisted of 17 reigns, ending in 1644. Power then passed to the Ch'ing (Qing) dynasty, which consisted of 11 reigns and lasted until 1916. Ming means 'bright' and Ch'ing (Qing) means 'pure'.

Chinese dynasties
Shang Yin 1760–1120 BCE
Chou 1120–249 BCE
Ch'in 221–206 BCE
Han 206 BCE – 220 CE
Six Dynasties 220–589 CE
T'ang 618–906 CE
Five Dynasties 907–960 CE
Sung 960–1279 CE
Yuan 1279–1367 CE
Ming 1368–1644 CE
Ch'ing 1644–1916 CE

JAPANESE PORCELAIN

Porcelain was first made in Japan in the early 17th century, beginning with the early Arita wares. Decoration, especially for export to Europe, often followed the Chinese style. However, there are a number of distinctive Japanese styles, among them Imari with its popular vivid red, blue and gilded vases and dishes; Kakiemon, with its beautiful enamel decoration; and Nabeshima, which used delicate underglaze blue and enamel decoration.

Japanese marks

Japanese marks are even more unreliable than Chinese ones. They include not only copies of Chinese marks, but names of potters, patrons and places. However, much of the best Japanese porcelain bears no marks at all, and very few marks appear before the end of the 18th century.
A few common examples of Japanese marks have been included here for reference.

'Kenzan' signature

Two forms of 'fuku' (meaning happiness)

'Raku' seal

'Banko' seal

'Kutani'

Impressed signature of 'Ninsei'

1 Hung-wu (Hongwu), 1368–98
2 Chien-wen, 1399–1402
3a Yung-lo (Yongle), 1403–24
3b 3a in archaic script
4 Hung-hsi, 1425
5a Hsuan-te (Xuande), 1426–35
5b 5a in seal characters
6 Cheng-t'ung, 1436–49
7 Ching-t'ai, 1450–57
8 T'ien-shun, 1457–64
9a Ch'eng-hua, 1465–87
9b 9a in seal characters
10 Hung-chih (Hongzhi), 1488–1505
11 Cheng-te (Zhengde), 1506–21
12 Chia-ching (Jiajing), 1522–66
13 Lung-ch'ing (Longqing), 1567–72
14 Wan-li (Wanli), 1573–1619
15 T'ai-ch'ang, 1620
16 Tien-ch'i (Tianqi), 1621–27
17 Ch'ung-cheng (Chongzhen), 1628–43

Ming dynasty reign marks

1 洪武年製

2 建文

3a 永樂年製

3b 永樂年製

4 洪熙

5a 大明宣德年製

5b 大明宣德年製

6 正統

7 景泰

8 天順

9a 大明成化年製

9b 成化年製

10 大明弘治年製

11 大明正德年製

12 大明嘉靖年製

13 大明隆慶年製

14 大明萬曆年製

15 泰昌

16 大明天啟年製

17 崇禎年製

Ch'ing (Qing) dynasty

1 大清順治年製

2 大清康熙年製

3 大清雍正年製

4 大清乾隆年製

5 崇禎年製

6 大清道光年製

7 大清咸豐年製

8 大清同治年製

9 大清光緒年製

10 大清宣統年製

11 洪憲年製

1 Shun-chih (Shunzhi), 1644–61
2 K'ang-hsi (Kangxi), 1662–1722
3 Yung-cheng (Yongzheng), 1723–35
4 Ch'ien-lung (Qianlong), 1736–95
5 Chia-ch'ing (Jiaqing), 1796–1821
6 Tao-kung (Daoguang), 1821–50
7 Hsien-feng (Xianfeng), 1851–61
8 T'ung-chih (Tongzhi), 1862–73
9 Kuang-hsu (Guangxu), 1874–1908
10 Hsuan-t'ung (Xuantong), 1909–12
11 Hung-hsien (Hongxian), 1916

Ceramic terminology

alkaline glaze Glaze containing soda or potash which, when small quantities of copper oxide are present, gives a rich turquoise colour.

applied relief See **sprigging**

biscuit (bisque) Pottery or porcelain clay which has been fired once without a glaze so that it is hard but porous and still has original clay colour.

biscuit painting or printing Designs applied directly to the unglazed biscuit.

biscuit porcelain Ware heated to a temperature high enough to decompose the clay and produce a porous biscuit.

body and **paste** General terms for the various clays from which pots are made. Body is generally used when referring to earthenware or stoneware, paste when referring to porcelain or bone china.

bone china Usually termed 'china', a hard-paste porcelain made from china clay and china stone, made white and strong by the addition of bone-ash from ox bones.

bone porcelain Soft-paste porcelain body strengthened with powdered bone ash.

brownware Brown, salt-glazed stoneware.

burnishing Rubbing the surface of an unfired pot with a smooth-surfaced tool; the particles of clay, pressed flat and smooth, take on a dull gloss.

cabinet ware Decorative pieces intended for display only.

Dresden cabinet ware

casting Process of shaping a ceramic object by pouring slip into a dry plaster mould; the mould absorbs water from the slip leaving a layer of clay on the inner surface of the mould; when the clay is of the correct thickness, the surplus is poured off and the object dries and shrinks to become cheese-hard, enabling it to be removed from the mould. Casting is used to make shapes that cannot be thrown on a potter's wheel.

ceramic ware Term for all fired clays, including pottery and porcelain.

cheese-hard Describes clay that is still soft enough to be worked.

china Common term for porcelain, first used in the 18th century. When imported Chinese porcelain was known as 'China ware', to distinguish it from earthenware.

china clay Pure kaolin or white clay, essential for the production of porcelain.

china stone Form of feldspar used in porcelain production; known in China as pai-tun-tzu (petuntse); also known as Cornish stone.

chinoiserie European decoration inspired by oriental sources.

clay Plastic, malleable earth used to make pots.

colouring oxides Metal oxides which, when painted onto or mixed into a glaze, give different colours.

combing Incised parallel-line decoration made by a toothed tool such as a comb.

creamware Earthenware with a cream-coloured glaze, fired at a moderate temperature, often plain or simply decorated; also known as Queensware.

delftware Tin-glazed earthenware, originally made in Delft, Holland.

dry edge Base of a figurine or pot left dry and unglazed.

earthenware Pottery fired at temperatures up to 1150°C, in which glaze and body remain as quite separate layers.

enamels Glazes prepared in frit form to melt at a low temperature, allowing a wide range of colours, which are then painted onto a fired glaze and refired in a muffle kiln; also known as on-glaze decoration.

Enamel Limoges dish

engine-turned decoration Incised decoration done on unfired leather-hard pottery with the aid of an engine-turned lathe.

faïence Tin-glazed earthenware, originally named after pottery coming from Faenza, Italy.

feldspar Naturally occurring mineral consisting of aluminium, silica and a flux of potassium or sodium; melts at 1250°C to form a simple glaze.

fettling Process of finishing a cast pot before firing by removing any marks and blemishes left by the cast with a metal tool.

firing Baking clay in a kiln at high temperature to transform it into pottery or porcelain, or baking glazed ware to fix the glaze. Twice-fired means baking pottery or porcelain again to fix the painting or decoration on once-fired ware.

flux Essential ingredient of glaze that causes other ingredients to melt and fuse to form the glaze; different fluxes affect colouring oxides to give a wide range of colours.

frit Artificially produced body material or glaze made by heating two or more raw materials together until they are fused or fritted, then grinding to a powder and mixing with clay to form a body for use.

glaze Smooth, non-porous, glossy coating made from silicate or glass-based substances applied to pots as a powder or in suspension in water.

glost kiln Kiln in which glazed ware receives its second, less intense firing to fuse the glaze.

hard-paste (true) porcelain Pure white porcelain made from china clay and china stone and given great strength despite its apparent delicacy by ageing the paste. It is called 'hard-paste' because it requires a 'hard fire', at a high temperature of around 1450°C.

high-temperature colours Those colours such as cobalt blue, manganese purple and iron red, that can be painted on the unfired surface of porcelain and that are capable of withstanding the full heat of a kiln.

impressing Pressing a maker's mark into the unfired clay with a stamp.
incised decoration Decoration pressed or cut into the surface of a pot.
incising Scratching a maker's mark into the clay before firing.
ironstone Hard, white earthenware strengthened with the ground-down top layer of molten slag from a blast furnace.
jackfield ware Generic term for any ware glazed with a glossy black finish. First made at Jackfield, Shropshire in the 18th century; also called jetware.
jasper Fine-grained stoneware, usually unglazed, and coloured with various materials to form a hard body.
kiln Potter's oven in which the fire is kept separate from the chamber holding the pots.
lead glaze Powdered lead ore sprinkled on ware that turns yellow when fired.
leather-hard Halfway stage between wet and dry clay, stiff enough to support its own weight but sufficiently pliable to bend slightly and be carved.
levigation Process of preparing fine particle-size clay by reducing the clay to liquid and decanting the finer particles that remain in suspension while the heavier particles sink to the bottom.
low relief Decoration slightly raised from the surface.
lustre Type of coloured decoration achieved by painting metallic pigment onto a fired glaze and refiring it to give an iridescent effect.
luting Process of cementing two parts of a ceramic object, such as a handle and a cup, with fluid clay slip; the joint is made less visible through fettling. 
majolica (maiolica) General term for tin-glazed earthenware decorated with oxides painted on to the unfired glaze; first made in 15th-century Italy, but term used specifically in the 19th century for moulded earthenware decorated with coloured glazes or majolica painting.
modelling Making the original wax or clay design required to shape the master mould.
monochrome pottery Pottery usually made in one colour or that has decoration painted in one colour.

Majolica pilgrim's bottle

moulding Process of shaping tableware and figures by pressing the clay or porcelain body into a mould, a process that allows multiple copies to be produced. Moulded pieces are often made in several parts and then joined together by luting.
moons or **grease spots** Small discs of higher translucency than the main body of some soft-paste porcelains; caused by imperfect blending of the ingredients.
muffle kiln Flame-burning kiln that protects pots from flames; essential for the production of enamels.
natron Mineral containing sodium oxide that acts as a flux in a glaze or faïence.
opacifier Substance, usually a metal oxide such as tin oxide, which, when added to clear glazes, suspends itself and renders a glaze opaque and white.
ornamenting Relief decoration shaped in a

separate mould and sprigged to the surface of the pot before firing.

overglaze mark Maker's mark painted, transfer-printed or stencilled onto a finished piece.

oxidizing atmosphere Conditions inside a kiln when a clean, bright flame burns with plenty of oxygen available, often producing bright red pots and yellow or brown iron-glazes. A reducing atmosphere, its opposite, is when oxygen content is kept to a minimum by burning damp fuel or closing air inlets, often producing dark brown or black pots and green or blue iron-glazes.

paddle and anvil Tools used for hand-made pottery. The anvil, often a stone, supports the pot wall while the paddle is beaten against the outside wall to shape it.

parian ware Unglazed, white, soft-paste porcelain with a characteristic silkiness, often used for figurines.

paste See **body**

pipeclay Fine white substance made from china clay and used as decoration.

plastic Describes clay that can be moulded without breaking.

porcelain White, translucent ware made by mixing china clay and china stone together to form the body, which is then fired at high temperature. There are three main types of porcelain: hard-paste or true porcelain, soft-paste or artificial porcelain and bone china.

potash Form of potassium oxide found in wood ash; acts as a flux in faïence or a glaze.

pottery Generic term for all ceramic wares. In normal use, all wares that are not porcelain.

potter's wheel Horizontal wheel that revolves on a vertical spindle used for throwing and turning pots.

pressing Process of shaping clay by pressing it into a press mould.

quartz Form of silica, such as sand, which when mixed with a suitable flux will form a glaze.

reducing atmosphere See **oxidizing atmosphere**

registered design mark Diamond-shaped mark required by the British Patent Office from 1842 to 1883 on all manufactured goods, including porcelain, showing the year, month and day of registration. From 1884 onwards the diamond mark was replaced by the simple registration numbering system still in use today.

Porcelain vase

raku Japanese lead-glazed pottery fired at a very low temperature.

relief Raised decoration modelled onto the pottery or porcelain body.

resist Decoration where one area is painted with a wax substance that resists colouring pigment or glaze when applied to the pot and therefore fires a contrasting colour.

saggar Covered box of baked fireclay in which potters pack fine ceramics in a kiln to protect them from the flames.

saltglaze Thin glaze achieved by

introducing salt into a high-temperature kiln; the chlorine escapes while the sodium vapour forms a glaze on the surface of the pot.

sgraffito Decoration scratched through a layer of slip to show the body, which has a contrasting colour.

slip Clay that has been softened in water to the consistency of cream and put through a sieve to make it smooth.

slip-cast ware Pottery and porcelain made by casting.

slipware Plain earthenware decorated with slip and then glazed.

soapstone porcelain Soft-paste porcelain that bridges the gap between earthenware and bone china.

soft-paste (artificial) porcelain Translucent white porcelain made by firing white clay with a frit of usually alum, gypsum, nitre, salt, soda and white sand melted together in a glassy mass, then pulverised and ground down. Called soft-paste because of the soft or low firing temperature of around 1200°C.

sprigging Decorating technique in which relief-moulded decoration is applied to a leather-hard pot, slightly raised on the surface.

spur marks Marks left on the underside of the ware by the points of spurs or stilts separating the pieces in a saggar when they are fired.

stoneware Strong non-porous ware made from adding sand or flint to the clay; when fired at a high temperature (1350°C), the clay is vitrified and the glaze and body partially fused, making it as hard as stone, hence its name.

terracotta Unglazed, slightly porous earthenware made of reddish clay and lightly fired.

throwing Art of building up a pot on a fast-spinning potter's wheel using centrifugal force.

tin glaze Glaze made white and opaque by the addition of tin oxide; also known as tin enamel, as the glaze resembles white enamel paint.

Slip-cast ware

transfer printing Process of decorating ceramic ware by inking an engraved copper plate with an ink prepared from a metallic oxide, then transferring the design to paper and when still wet onto the ware; it is fixed by firing.

turning Process of removing surplus clay from a thrown pot by returning the leather-hard pot to the wheel and trimming it with a metal tool.

underglaze mark Maker's mark created with paint or transfer before the final glaze is applied over it.

underglaze painting Technique of painting colouring oxides onto unfired pottery that may or may not be subsequently glazed.

viscous Glaze which when melted remains stiff and does not run down the pot.

vitrified Literally, like glass, fused together.

weathering Clay intended for good-quality porcelain and earthenware is weathered in the rain, Sun and frost for a year to remove undesirable salts, break it down and dry it for handling.

Need to know more?

Books
Miller's Silver and Plate Buyer's Guide
Edited by Daniel Bexfield, Miller's, 2002
The Price Guide to Antique Silver
Peter Waldron, Antique Collectors' Club Ltd, 2001
Starting to Collect Antique Silver
Ian Pickford, Antique Collectors' Club Ltd, 2003
Miller's Ceramics Buyer's Guide
Edited by Chris Spencer, Miller's, 2000
Blue and White Pottery: A Collector's Guide
Gillian Neale, Miller's, 2000

Websites
BBC Antiques
BBC website devoted to antiques on television, radio and in your local areas, with price and collectors' guides
www.bbc.co.uk/antiques/
Antiques UK
Contains directories of dealers, collectors, fairs, auctions, clubs and trade associations in the UK and elsewhere in the world
www.antiques-uk.co.uk
Antique British Ceramics Information Resource
An information base for British potteries, their products and workforce
www.abcir.org

Clubs
Clarice Cliff Collectors' Club
Fantasque House, Tennis Drive, The Park
Nottingham NG7 1AE
www.claricecliff.com

Oriental Ceramics Society
Supports knowledge and understanding of oriental ceramics and provides a valuable link between collectors, curators, and others
Secretary/Administrator Mrs Jean Martin
30b Torrington Square
London WC1E 7JL
Tel: 020 7636 7985
Email: osclondon@beeb.net
www.ocs_london.members.beeb.net

Royal Doulton International Collectors Club
Gives you direct access to Royal Doulton and opens up a whole new world of beautiful china and other collectables
Sir Henry Doulton House
Forge Lane, Etruria
Stoke-on-Trent ST1 5NN
Tel: 01782 404046
Email: icc@royal-doulton.com
www.royal-doulton.com

The Silver Society
Box 246
2 Lansdowne Row
London W1J 6HL
Email: info@thesilversociety.org
www.thesilversociety.org

Silver Spoon Club of Great Britain
Supports and assists connoisseurs and collectors of antiques and other fine silver spoons
26 Burlington Arcade,
Mayfair, London W1J OPU
Tel: 020 7491 1720
Email: silverspoonclub
www.bexfield.co.uk/thefinial

The Spode Society
The Curator
c/o Spode Museum
Spode
Church Street
Stoke-on-Trent ST4 1BX
Tel: 01782 744011
Email: spodemuseum@spode.co.uk
www.spode.co.uk

The Wedgwood Society of Great Britain
89 Andrewes House
Barbican
London EC2Y 8AY
Tel: 020 7628 7268

Index

Applying colour, ceramics 178

Carat 17
Casting, precious metal 120
Ceramics 122-188
Ceramics, surface work 178-179
Chain making, precious metal 118
Chenier work, precious metal 121
Coiled pottery, methods of construction 174
Convention marks, precious metal 15, 22

Damascene work, precious metal 116
Date letters 12, 14
Date letters, sample 12
Duty marks 13

Filigree work, precious metal 121

Gold, African 86-87
Gold, American 84-85
Gold, Indian colonial 88-89
Goldsmiths 90-94

Hallmarking Act 1973 14
Hallmarking Council, British 15
Hallmarks on silver 11
Hallmarks, current international 22
Hallmarks, current UK, gold 20
Hallmarks, current UK, platinum 21
Hallmarks, current UK, silver 16
Hallmarks, how to read 24
Hallmarks, pre-1975 10
Hallmarks, reading the charts 24
Hallmarks, silver, gold, platinum 10
Hallmarks, silver, sample 11

Maker's marks, Birmingham 77
Maker's marks, Chester 68
Maker's marks, Dublin 59
Maker's marks, Edinburgh 41
Maker's marks, Exeter 52
Maker's marks, Glasgow 72
Maker's marks, London 33-34
Maker's marks, Newcastle 63
Maker's marks, Sheffield 83
Maker's marks, York 46
Manufacturers, pottery and porcelain 168 -173
Mark, Assay Office 16, 22, 23
Mark, metal and fineness, gold 20
Mark, metal and fineness, platinum 22
Mark, metal and fineness, silver 16
Mark, sponsor's and maker's, platinum 21
Mark, sponsor's and maker's, gold 20
Mark, sponsor's and maker's, silver 16
Marks of origin on British silver to 1974 11
Marks of origin from 1975 14
Marks of origin on imported gold 19
Marks, ceramic makers' 127-167
Marks, ceramics, anchors 149
Marks, ceramics, animals, fishes and insects 150
Marks, ceramics, arrows 151
Marks, ceramics, birds 152
Marks, ceramics, circles 153
Marks, ceramics, crescents 154
Marks, ceramics, crossed swords 156
Marks, ceramics, crowns 157

Marks, ceramics, curves 158
Marks, ceramics, fleurs-de-lys 159
Marks, ceramics, flowers and trees 160
Marks, ceramics, lines and crosses 155
Marks, ceramics, miscellaneous 166–167
Marks, ceramics, oriental copies 165
Marks, ceramics, shields 161
Marks, ceramics, squares 162
Marks, ceramics, stars and suns 163
Marks, ceramics, triangles and hearts 164
Marks, Chinese porcelain 180–183
Marks, commemorative 13
Marks, compulsory, gold 20
Marks, compulsory, platinum 21
Marks, compulsory, silver 16
Marks, foreign silver, to 1974 13
Marks, foreign, British and Irish gold 19
Marks, Japanese porcelain 181
Marks, makers' 11
Marks, makers', sample 12
Marks, methods of applying, pottery 125
Marks, Old Sheffield Plate 102–109
Marks, other, gold 19
Marks, other, pewter 111
Marks, quality, pewter 110
Marks, registered design, ceramics 126
Marks, silver, standard 14
Marks, silver, standard to 1974 12
Marks, silver, standard, sample 12
Marks, standard on British gold 17
Marks, standard on imported gold 19
Marks, standard on Irish gold 18
Marks, standard under the Act 1973 18
Marks, touch, pewter 111
Marks, touch, sample 111
Methods of construction, ceramics 174–177
Month codes 1842-83, ceramics 126
Moulded pottery, methods of construction 176

Oriental porcelain 180–183

Pewter 110
Pierced work, precious metal 119
Porcelain types 125
Porcelain, Chinese 180–183
Porcelain, Japanese 181
Pottery and porcelain 124–188
Pottery types 124
Precious metal working 114
Precious metals 8–99
Punch tools, Native American, precious metal 117
Raku pottery, methods of construction 177
Registration numbers, ceramics 126
Relief tools, ceramics 179
Repoussé work, precious metal 118–119

Sheffield Plate, Old 102
Silver, American 84–85
Silver, imported foreign from 1975 15
Silver, Indian colonial 88–89
Silversmiths 90–94

Terminology, ceramic 184–188
Terminology, goldsmiths' 95–99
Terminology, silversmiths' 95–99
Thrown pottery, methods of construction 175
Tools and techniques, precious metal 114–115
Touchplates, sample marks 112–113

Collins need to know?

Look out for further titles in Collins' practical and accessible need to know? series.

To order any of these titles, please telephone 0870 787 1732.

For further information on Collins books, please visit our website: www.collins.co.uk